10-Minute CBT

10-Minute CBT

Integrating Cognitive-Behavioral Strategies into Your Practice

Michael W. Otto

Naomi M. Simon

Bunmi O. Olatunji

Sharon C. Sung

Mark H. Pollack

OXFORD
UNIVERSITY PRESS

OXFORD
UNIVERSITY PRESS

Oxford University Press, Inc., publishes works that further
Oxford University's objective of excellence
in research, scholarship, and education.

Oxford   New York
Auckland   Cape Town   Dar es Salaam   Hong Kong   Karachi
Kuala Lumpur   Madrid   Melbourne   Mexico City   Nairobi
New Delhi   Shanghai   Taipei   Toronto

With offices in
Argentina   Austria   Brazil   Chile   Czech Republic   France   Greece
Guatemala   Hungary   Italy   Japan   Poland   Portugal   Singapore
South Korea   Switzerland   Thailand   Turkey   Ukraine   Vietnam

Copyright © 2011 by Oxford University Press, Inc.

Published by Oxford University Press, Inc.
198 Madison Avenue, New York, New York 10016
www.oup.com

Oxford is a registered trademark of Oxford University Press

Library of Congress Cataloging-in-Publication Data

10-minute CBT: integrating cognitive-behavioral strategies into your practice / Michael W. Otto ... [et al.].
p.; cm.
Ten-minute CBT
10-minute cognitive-behavioral therapy
Includes bibliographical references.
ISBN 978-0-19-533974-1
1. Cognitive therapy. I. Otto, Michael W. II. Title: Ten-minute CBT. III. Title: 10-minute cognitive-behavioral
therapy.
[DNLM: 1. Cognitive Therapy—methods. 2. Anxiety Disorders—therapy. 3. Depressive Disorder—therapy.
4. Sleep Initiation and Maintenance Disorders—therapy. WM 425.5.C6]
RC489.C63.A14 2010
616.89'1425—dc22   2010045914

9 8 7 6 5 4 3 2 1
Printed in the United States of America
on acid-free paper

M.W.O.:   To my son, Jackson, who charms me daily.

N.M.S.:   To my mother Hannah, who introduced me to the field of mental health, and who has helped me juggle the demands of career and motherhood.

B.O.O.:   To my loving parents, Francis and Christianah.

S.C.S.:   To my husband, Zack, for your love and support I am continuously grateful.

M.H.P.:   To Patty, Josh, and JJ, the lights of my life.

CONTENTS

ACKNOWLEDGMENTS

The authors would like to thank the Highland Street Foundation for their support and encouragement of this project, and the work they do to improve the lives of so many.

10-Minute CBT

1

INTRODUCTION

It is difficult to write a book that reduces the richness of cognitive-behavioral therapy (CBT) down to select interventions to be offered in a component fashion. But the demand for this book was just that. To address the request: "Just tell me what to do in my clinical visits so that my patients can get at least a modicum of CBT." This approach differs substantially from the session-by-session manual-based approaches that have largely defined the field. We have written treatment manuals in that format (e.g., Otto et al., 2009, Otto & Pollack, 2009) and find them valuable, but offering up a principle-based treatment is a welcomed alternative. We are aware, from our time spent training professionals in presentations and workshops, that many clinicians are uncomfortable with or are unable to effect a wholesale change in the type of treatment they are currently providing. They would like to incorporate CBT elements, but the nature of their practice makes them hesitant to switch to the prescribed session-by-session format that is offered by most current treatment manuals. As such, one benefit of the *10-Minute CBT* approach is that it presents CBT in a way that makes it easy for clinicians from any interventional perspective (psychopharmacologic, dynamic, supportive, etc.) to incorporate elements of CBT into their practice. Instead of providing a full regimented program of treatment, we provide the philosophy and elements of treatment so that select interventions can be integrated into an existing pharmacotherapy or psychotherapy program.

Despite this obvious benefit, the process of boiling down CBT into an elixir of brief components made us uneasy—will it make CBT appear to be too simplistic? What about the richness and the programmatic learning that are at the heart of CBT? Will that be lost as it is divided into easily digested units? Our response to these concerns was to separate our discussion of the conceptual richness of CBT from our presentation of interventions that can be taken "one teaspoon at a time." We devoted Chapters 2 to 5 to elucidating the "feel" and principles of treatment, to free us up to provide a more mechanistic summary of component interventions in the disorder-specific sections that follow. Nonetheless, we have also included some stylistic examples in these latter chapters, with examples of how an intervention may appear in practice by providing patient/clinician dialogues. Because we separated discussion of principles of treatment from discussion of components of treatment, we hope that the readers of this manual will use the principles of change and stylistic considerations from Chapters 2 to 5 to shape the component interventions they provide. Also, the disorder-specific chapters are of different lengths. Greatest detail was provided for the first two chapters, panic disorder and major depression, with subsequent chapters drawing from the examples and principles provided in these chapters and Chapters 2 to 5.

As empirically minded clinicians, we also could not feel comfortable leaving out the evidence behind CBT approaches. We considered writing a chapter summarizing just how acceptable and efficacious CBT is for anxiety, mood, and sleep disorders, but this is not the sort of information desired by those seeking clear information on component interventions for the next session. Nonetheless, we wanted to provide readers with more specific findings supporting some of the principles of change and component interventions that we review in subsequent chapters. For this reason, we also provided "Academic Moment" boxes throughout the chapters to give background information with appropriate references. For clinicians wishing to focus specifically on interventions, these Academic Moment boxes can be overlooked in favor of the directly clinical material. For other readers, these informational boxes will provide the desired background useful for a more complete understanding of some of the intellectual heritage behind the principle or intervention being illustrated.

In addition, we adhered to one final principle of dissemination appropriate for busy clinicians: keep it short. Accordingly, let's get started.

2

PROVIDING CBT

ORIENTING THE PATIENT TO TREATMENT

Cognitive-behavioral therapy (CBT) is an especially active treatment for both the patient and provider, with the goal of full cessation of the patient's symptoms. The strategy for achieving this outcome is the step-by-step elimination of cognitive, emotional, and behavioral patterns that maintain disorders. During treatment the patient will be asked to learn and practice new strategies, with the clinician in the role of an expert and guide who knows the nature of disorders, the nature of the change process, and the importance of supporting individuals emotionally as they work to develop new strategies in relation to painful aspects of their lives.

Patients who have been in supportive or dynamic therapy need to be reoriented to the here-and-now focus of CBT and the programmed change process in which each week builds on the content, practice, and implementation of strategies from the previous week. Indeed, much of the style of CBT shares greater commonalities with pharmacotherapy than dynamic psychotherapy. As with pharmacotherapy, disorders are viewed syndromally, and interventions are matched to the underlying disorder. Likewise, the clinician is in the role of the expert who is explicitly going to offer the patient active interventions that will require his or her between-session efforts (e.g., regular pill-taking in the case of pharmacotherapy, completion of home practice assignments in the case of CBT). Accurate diagnosis, therapist warmth, clear communications, ongoing monitoring, and a devotion to the patient's needs provide the frame for these interventions.

PATIENT EFFORT

At the outset of this book, it is important to dispel the myth that CBT is particularly difficult for patients to undergo, and that few patients are able to tolerate the procedures required to get better. As judged by research on anxiety disorders, this notion is far from the truth. When CBT is accurately described to patients, it is typically a fully acceptable intervention, with more patients electing to engage in CBT than in pharmacotherapy (Hofmann et al., 1998), fewer dropouts once treatment is initiated (see McHugh, Smits & Otto, 2009), and high alliance ratings relative to alternative treatments (see Halperin, Weitzman & Otto, 2009). Nonetheless, CBT does ask for particularly active involvement from patients, and it is important to review some of the elements of CBT that may be especially helpful for encouraging patients to enter into and stay with treatment.

PROVIDING A VISION OF THE PROBLEM

One common element of CBT across disorders is the provision of patients with understandable models of their disorder and the change process. These models are presented in everyday language, most often in terms of chains of thoughts, feelings, and behaviors. Emphasis is placed on the patterns that maintain disorders, and correspondingly on strategies to eliminate these patterns. This involves active learning of alternative patterns, and throughout treatment it will be important to provide patients with a vision of the changes they will be making. If done well, the focus will not simply be on the reduction of psychopathology, but on the enhancement of well-being. For example, for the treatment of panic disorder, the focus is not simply on the elimination of panic attacks, but on the return to desired functioning. To achieve this focus, at the outset of treatment the clinician should help the patient create a vision of recovery by asking such questions as:

• What will you be doing when you are better?
• What are some things you might be doing that you are not doing now?
• What will an average day be like when you are better?
• What do you think you will be doing as well as feeling?

These questions help the patient translate a general goal such as "to feel better" into a more specific and richer set of life goals that provides greater guidance on the change process and provides "signposts" of recovery for the patient.

If the signposts of recovery provide the patient with ways to mark his or her progress and translate general efforts into specific goals, the CBT model of the disorder is designed to provide the patient with an opportunity to better mobilize his or her problem-solving efforts in the service of recovery. As clinicians well know, understanding the disorder is different from treating it effectively and, as such, treatment is aimed at providing patients with the experiences they need to make lasting changes to their maladaptive patterns. At the clinician's disposal are a wide range of programmed interventions, including self-monitoring with corrective feedback, rehearsal of component skills, activity assignments, and active role-playing of skills, along with carefully designed exposure assignments and behavioral experiments that allow the patient to learn from his or her own ongoing experiences in high-emotion situations.

Box 2.1 Academic Moment: Therapeutic Alliance

Although the effect is frequently modest, a strong therapeutic alliance is nonetheless associated with better outcomes in treatment (for review, see Martin et al., 2000). Alliance has been most commonly conceptualized in terms of three central factors: the goals, tasks, and bonds of therapy. *Goals* refer to the desired outcomes identified by both patient and clinician, and in CBT these goals are to be made explicit, with monitoring of progress toward these goals across short-term treatment. *Tasks* are specific to a clinician's theoretical orientation; in CBT the tasks of therapy are tailored to providing patients with the necessary training to eliminate maladaptive patterns. Finally, *bonds* refers to the attachment and trust between clinician and patient. None of these variables are static, and it is clear that efforts devoted to clarifying goals and defining therapeutic tasks have clear payoffs for the patient's engagement and achievement in treatment. For example, a study of individuals who had previously refused exposure treatment for obsessive-compulsive disorder examined the effect of a 4-session readiness intervention provided before these patients were again offered 15 sessions of exposure treatment (Maltby & Tolin, 2005) and found that 86% of patients undergoing the readiness condition accepted exposure treatment, compared to only 20% for a waitlist condition. Also, given the general association between CBT homework adherence and treatment outcome for the anxiety disorders (Westra, Dozois & Marcus, 2007; but compare Woods, Chambless & Steketee, 2002), it may be particularly important to help patients form accurate expectations for an active treatment role. Such expectancies can be altered with information, including the use of pretreatment audio and video tapes and instructional brochures (Bonner & Everett, 1982; Day & Reznikoff, 1980; Shuman & Shapiro, 2002).

In all of these therapeutic activities, there is a focus on having patients learn about their patterns and the change process so that over time they become experts in their own treatment. The goal is not to have patients end therapy after short-term treatment, but to become their own therapist and take over treatment. As such, the goal of the clinician is to work to become redundant with the patient's own treatment efforts. Thus, patients can stop attending regular sessions when they *can provide for themselves what the clinician used to provide.*

As part of this process, it is important for patients to know what works and what does not work when intervening with their disorder. Regular self-monitoring of symptoms helps the patient identify progress when it occurs, and one role for the clinician is to draw attention to the link between the patient's efforts and these improvements. For this reason, we prefer, when at all possible, for CBT to occur against a backdrop of stable medication use. If the clinician varies two treatment modalities at once, it may be unclear which led to the improvements being achieved. Whereas the identification of the most efficacious treatment may not be important to the patient acutely, the attribution of treatment gains (see Academic Moment, Box 2.2) does have important implications for rates of relapse. For instance, patients attributing their improvement to pharmacotherapy may be at greater risk for relapse following medication discontinuation than individuals who associate improvement with the application of cognitive-behavioral techniques that they can continue to apply even after the course of formal sessions with a therapist has ended. If CBT interventions are initiated during pharmacotherapy interventions or changes, it is important to stress that utilization of CBT approaches will help the patient gain control over affect and function, and to be aware that additional CBT intervention may be needed once medication is stabilized. With the correct identification of helpful skills and strategies, it is our hope that patients will learn to appropriately apply therapy principles and interventions to future as well as current distress.

Box 2.2 Academic Moment: Attribution of Treatment Gains

A study by Powers and associates (2008) offers a particularly clear example of the potential negative effects of attribution of treatment gains to a pill rather than to personal effort. In their study, participants were randomized to a waitlist control condition, a psychological placebo condition, a single-session exposure-based treatment, or a single-session exposure-based treatment in conjunction with an inactive pill, where patients' expectations of the pill's effects were manipulated in one of three ways. Participants in the exposure-plus-pill group were led to believe that the pill they were given was either a sedating herbal supplement with anxiety-dampening effects, a stimulating herbal supplement with anxiogenic effects, or a placebo pill that did not affect exposure treatment. Results of the study indicated that participants who were led to believe that they took a sedating herb rated the pill as being more helpful than those who were told that they had taken the stimulating herb or one without effect. Additionally, participants who believed that they had taken an herbal stimulant (that made the exposure more difficult) rated the pill as hindering their treatment more than the other groups did. However, the most important effects, predicted by the investigators, were that participants who were told after treatment that they had taken a sedating herb (that dampened their anxiety) had a significantly higher return of fear at a one-week follow-up. More importantly, participants in the exposure-plus-sedating-herb condition no longer out-performed the waitlist or psychological placebo condition at the follow-up evaluation, while the other three exposure conditions (e.g., exposure alone, exposure plus a pill described as a stimulating herb, and exposure plus a pill described as a placebo) maintained improvement over the waitlist and psychological placebo conditions.

These findings are consistent with studies of panic disorder showing that individuals who attributed their improvement in treatment to a medication were at risk of poorer mainte-nance of treatment gains in panic disorder (Basoglu, Marks, Kilic, Brewin & Swinson, 1994; Biondi & Picardi, 2003), posttraumatic stress disorder (see Ehlers, Mayou & Bryant, 1998), agoraphobia (Chambless & Gracely, 1989), and obsessive-compulsive disorder (Basoglu, Lax, Kasvikis & Marks, 1988).

ORIENTING THE PATIENT TO THE CHANGE PROCESS

As dysfunctional as they may be, many maladaptive patterns feel comfortable to patients: they are part of each patient's known repertoire. For this reason, adaptive change may leave patients with feelings of discomfort during the week between sessions. For this reason it is helpful to prepare patients for both the effort required in therapy (practicing new ways of being) and the way adaptive changes may feel—in many cases, individuals may at first feel emotionally "off balance." Helping patients to persist should new patterns feel odd ("if you feel odd this week, this might be an important signpost of useful change") can help them maintain new patterns rather than reverting to habitual and maladaptive, albeit more comfortable, behaviors.

In its most basic form, behavior therapy asks patients to resist the natural dysfunc-tional behaviors that are driven by their disorder. For example, depression makes one feel like doing less, and anxiety drives avoidance and vigilance. CBT approaches for these disorders encourage accurate identification and tolerance of these emotions while engaging in behaviors that help end these maladaptive patterns—activity and engagement. To help patients orient themselves to this approach, clinicians may say something like the following:

> *The general style of treatment with me may be different from what you have had in the past. In this treatment, I am going to be fairly active; that is, in certain sessions I may talk a lot. It is*

partly the goal of this treatment to teach you about common patterns associated with your disorder and how to shut down these patterns. This means that our therapy will involve more than talking, it will involve DOING. In short, we will be discussing emotional, thought, and behavioral patterns that either serve you well or impair your mood and functioning. Our goal is to increase the patterns that help you and decrease the patterns that hurt you through discussion and active practice.

ORGANIZATION OF THE SESSION

To allow the step-by-step building upon skills and new behavioral patterns rehearsed in the previous session, each session should include a review of successes and difficulties with the previous session content and assignments. After review, we encourage active setting of a single agenda item for the session, with at least one review or rehearsal of the concept. Subsequently, in transitioning to what is to be practiced out of session, we recommend asking the following questions of the patient:

1. How would you summarize what you need to apply from this session?

This question is designed to have the patient put the primary task in his or her own words; this should aid memory consolidation while providing the clinician with the ability to provide some correction should the patient have misunderstood the home practice assignment.

2. What might get in the way of practicing this over the next week?

This question is designed to acknowledge that home practice is hard, and to orient the patient toward overcoming common weekly obstacles to step-by-step practice.

3. What do you suppose you will be thinking when you go to try this for the first time?

This question is aimed at helping the patient overcome the negative thinking patterns that almost invariably accompany trying something new, different, or threatening.

We recognize that asking all three questions may be a slow process for some patients, and that clinicians will have to orient patients both to expect these questions and to provide focused answers that can fit within a brief-session format.

BRIDGING THE GAP BETWEEN THE SESSION
AND REAL LIFE

A core aspect of CBT is the active programming of change, including a transfer of what is learned in treatment sessions to the moments in life when new responses are needed. One common belief across therapies is that the creation of new patterns of behavior requires a protected environment. Indeed, a core feature of the notion of therapeutic frame is to create an environment where patients feel free to discuss topics and act in ways distinct from their usual patterns, and apart from the social pressures of everyday life. This is an excellent format for the elicitation of new behaviors. But once these new behaviors have been elicited, the challenge is to help patients transfer these new ways of being into their daily life. If the therapeutic relationship is truly a "relationship like no other," then one can easily imagine that the transfer of what is learned in this relationship to everyday life can be challenging. Accordingly, attention is placed on aiding this transfer of skills. Indeed, the notion of home readings (patient workbooks) and home practice of therapy (e.g., exposure and activity assignments) is to make sure the gap between what occurs in session and what is needed out of session is effectively bridged.

A common strategy for creating this bridge is the sequential inclusion of cues from the patient's world in therapy. Imaginal review of homework assignments, specific role-plays, and the induction of emotion are all ways to bring into the session the relevant cues from the real world. Also, we would like to emphasize the following principle for treatment: anything you really want your patient to do, *first do it in session*. We believe that the clinician should always be alert to how challenging a shift in behavior can be for patients. A quick imaginal or role-play rehearsal—which provides a patient with a memory of an initial (successful) attempt at the new behavior—can be especially valuable in helping patients to follow through successfully with avoided, feared, or otherwise difficult behaviors. The role-play also helps patients create a distinct memory of what it feels like to try out new behaviors under the conditions of relevant cues. This memory is then there to guide patients as they face a similar challenging situation in real life.

The following simple questions can be used to help the patient better envision how it would be to apply a therapy skill in the home environment. These questions help the patient develop cues for that behavior (when, where, and how it will feel):

- When will you do it?
- Where will you be standing/sitting?
- How will you be feeling at that time?

- What might you be thinking?
- How will you remember to do the intervention?
- What will make it hard? What might make it easier?

INCREASING THE POSITIVE AS WELL AS DECREASING THE NEGATIVE

We want clinicians (and their patients) to be more than *psychopathology reducers*; we want them to be *well-being enhancers*. A focus on well-being is fully compatible with standard CBT; however, it addresses the other side of the CBT "coin." Whereas CBT directs primary attention on the reduction of patterns that maintain psychopathology, well-being therapy focuses on the enhancement of periods of contentment and happiness. A cognitive-behavioral therapist applying both strategies works to both reduce psychopathology and enhance well-being. The elemental tools of a well-being focus are the same as CBT and include cognitive restructuring, activity management (targeting mastery, pleasure, and skill development), assertiveness training, and problem solving. All of the elements are directed at enhancing periods of well-being identified by the patient.

A well-being focus can be initiated at any point in treatment with assignment of a "hedonic diary," where patients monitor the thoughts and events linked to periods of well-being. Specifically, patients are asked to find a regular evening time for diary entry, and to record the time in the past 24 hours where well-being was most experienced. This diary has four purposes: (1) it reminds patients that periods of well-being occur despite the presence of affective disturbances, (2) it helps patients to re-experience these periods of well-being as these events are recalled and transcribed, (3) it helps direct patients toward attending to and planning for these events as they occur in the next several days, and (4) it provides a valuable record of periods of enjoyment over time that can be reviewed and used for planning of future events. After the first week of diary use, recording becomes more active, with examination of thoughts surrounding these periods of well-being, and attention to understanding how thoughts can be used to help patients extend these periods of well-being. Patients are taught to apply the treatment elements presented in this manual—cognitive restructuring, activity assignments, and skills training—to help them better create, attend to, and enjoy periods of well-being. There is evidence that doing so is useful for both treating residual symptoms and protecting against relapse of both anxiety and mood disorders (for review see Ruini & Fava, 2009).

ENDING TREATMENT

We think of the process of ending formal treatment as an active period that is designed for relapse prevention. During this stage, the patient is asked to complete therapeutic activities more independently and with less regular input from the clinician. For example, we may remind the patient of the basic elements of the next session of treatment (e.g., review of home practice and symptoms in relation to a model of the disorder and identification of topics for skill practice, problem solving, or other rehearsals), but ask him or her to schedule a session independent of the therapist:

> *Next week, hold your regular session at 10 a.m., but don't come here. I would like you to run the session yourself, and then come report on how it went in a meeting with me in two weeks.*

This fading out of treatment sessions occurs in the context of active rehearsals by the patient in "taking over the job of the therapist" and provides an active opportunity to independently apply CBT interventions. In addition to reviewing progress with this process, therapists should also begin to identify high-risk times for the return of symptoms and to discuss what therapy skills the patient will want to reapply should those situations arise. Ideally, though free to return if necessary, patients leave the formal therapy with an understanding of the nature of their disorder and the treatment process and the ability to serve as their own therapist, applying the necessary interventions to maintain and extend gains made and wellness achieved.

3

COGNITIVE INTERVENTIONS

Thoughts, when accurate, are incredibly useful. We plan, we estimate, and we evaluate; thereby we have the chance to test myriad actions from the safety of our own minds. With this ability we reap the daily benefits of a hundred missteps avoided, and a score of good plans honed. From the ice cream we choose to the work and relationships we pursue, thinking and estimating serves us well. But what happens if our thinking and estimating goes wide of the mark? What happens if we overestimate the dangerousness of talking to our boss, of taking the trip, or of asking for what we need from family members? What happens if we decide that "trying is not worth it," that "it won't work out," or that "it is not safe to go out," when none of these things are true? One short answer is that disorders are created, worsened, or maintained. Indeed, it is to the correction of these thoughts, images, and expectations that cognitive restructuring is devoted.

Cognitive restructuring is based on the premise that feelings and behaviors are influenced by one's perception of events. When these perceptions are in error, or when they are driven by emotions rather than accurate evaluation, trouble results. In classic cognitive restructuring therapeutic interventions, thoughts are treated as hypotheses, and emphasis is placed on the development of more accurate thinking patterns. More importantly, cognitive restructuring helps patients take a step back from treating thoughts as *truth*, and remembering that thoughts are simply guesses about the world, and such guesses should be considered in relation to their usefulness. Useful for what? Useful for helping patients reach their personal goals.

Cognitive restructuring strategies include guided discussions, Socratic questioning, self-monitoring, behavioral experiments (realistic tests of specific cognitions), and, at times, story heuristics (see page 25–26) used to guide patients in their self-talk.

The use of behavioral experiments, where programmed experiences are used to test the accuracy of specific beliefs, underscores the reality that cognitive change does not need to rely on verbal argument. Instead, behavioral experiments use specific observations of reality to help individuals bring their cognitions in line with actual outcomes and to promote adaptive behaviors.

STRATEGIES FOR COGNITIVE RESTRUCTURING

We recommend a series of hierarchical interventions for therapists to pursue when providing cognitive restructuring interventions. The first is to instruct the patient in the importance of evaluating the accuracy of thoughts: to learn not to take thoughts so seriously, and to know that accurate or not, thoughts can have a powerful effect on emotion and motivation. One important element in instructing patients about the role of thought in disorders (see disorder-specific chapters) is encouraging patients to "listen in" on their thoughts in a new way—not to take their thoughts at face value and to slow down and examine their thought content, especially when they experience a change in emotion. This strategy emphasizes the automaticity of thoughts, and that cognitive restructuring is aimed, in part, at changing dysfunctional habits in thinking. At times these habits have been longstanding, and at times they have been shaped by the emergence of an Axis I disorder. Regardless of the source, active listening and evaluation of self-talk in an objective way is the goal.

We have termed one strategy for introducing this active monitoring and contemplation of thoughts "CEO (chief executive officer) thinking." To achieve CEO thinking, one must approach cognitions as if they were separate reports from different divisions in a large company. Just like an effective CEO, the patient should imagine herself sitting (preferably reclining in a leather executive chair) and contemplating the style and substance of incoming information from each division filing a report. To be effective in consolidating these reports for appropriate action, the CEO needs to be aware of the reporting biases that each division has: *Marketing* may be overly positive and demanding of more attention, *Consumer Relations* may be fretting about company inadequacies, *Production* may be overly positive or negative about capabilities, and *Research* may be biased toward a certain vision of the future. And each division head will report to the CEO in his or her prototypic voice, which may be pleading, berating, whiny, fearful, and so forth. The job of the CEO is to lean back in the mental executive chair, listen to the reports, seek to understand the biases of each division of the company reporting, and dispassionately choose the behavioral options that best serve the values of the company (the patient, that is). This is *mindful* contemplation of the nature and usefulness of thoughts, and when observing the reports from each part of the company, patients have a chance to observe the link between specific thoughts and associated emotions.

To help patients become really good at seeing this link, clinicians may want to introduce them to the concept of "marveling." *Marveling* refers to appreciating the emotional tone of thoughts without buying into that emotion. In short, marveling is a "check this out; look at what I'm saying to myself" attitude that helps patients be aware of the tone of their thoughts without necessarily acting in response to it. In terms of form and content, a marveling CEO might find herself saying, "Wow, look at how whiny the *Production* part of myself is when it doesn't get what it wants," or "Whew, is *Consumer Relations* REALLY calling my boyfriend a heartless and manipulative jerk, just because he's late for the movie?" To marvel well, patients need to fully appreciate the depth of the emotional message as an event ("Ouch, that is really a mean thing I'm saying to myself") while being understanding and inquisitive ("How did I ever learn that was an OK way to talk to myself?") and while remaining in the CEO position ("I am not going to act on that thought"). Such mindful contemplation of thoughts is at the heart of the first, and perhaps most important, step of cognitive restructuring.

Box 3.1 Academic Moment: Gaining Perspective

There is evidence that, regardless of the style of cognitive intervention, one benefit achieved by patients is a more metacognitive perspective on cognitions—in other words, thoughts are held more at a distance, with greater independence between thoughts and emotional responses to those thoughts. Specifically, Teasdale and colleagues (2002) found that regardless of whether Beckian cognitive therapy was provided or whether patients received a mindfulness-based intervention, greater metacognitive awareness (gaining greater distance from negative thoughts and feelings so that these thoughts are not seen as "necessarily valid reflections of reality;" p. 285, Teasdale et al., 2002) was achieved in therapy, and this ability to hold thoughts at an appropriate distance was linked to lower rates of relapse to depression.

In classic cognitive therapy, the second step in cognitive restructuring is assignment of self-monitoring of thoughts and evaluation of their accuracy. This is typically done with daily recording sheets, under the assumption that the formal process of writing out thoughts and emotions helps patients develop a more objective frame for evaluating their cognitive content. Specifically, the process of writing out a thought and seeing it in black and white on a page can help patients evaluate their thoughts more dispassionately. When thoughts are moving out of the dark recesses of the mind and into the light of the open page, errors in thoughts and assumptions can be more easily identified by most people.

Self-monitoring is directed toward thoughts associated with an emotional change. Upon detection of a change in emotion, patients are to examine both the external situation ("What is going on?") and the internal environment ("What have I been saying to myself?"). Ideally, this process is completed with a sense of empathy toward oneself: "I am feeling bad; how can I understand what is going on?" For depressed and anxious patients, attention may need to be devoted to their *amplifying cognitions*—those thoughts that amplify the aversiveness of emotional experiences. Self-blame for depressive symptoms (depression about depression) and anxiety about and catastrophic misinterpretations of anxiety symptoms (anxiety sensitivity) are two classic responses that amplify negative and anxious affect. The chapters on depression and panic disorder devote specific attention to helping patients undo these feed-forward cycles of negative evaluation and amplified negative affect.

In addition to learning about amplifying cognitions, patients can benefit from instruction in common cognitive errors. Table 3.1 provides a list of some of these common thinking errors and can be used as a handout to be reviewed in session to help patients understand the "sound" and "feel" of dysfunctional thoughts so they can better identify these thoughts when they occur. By providing patients with a classification system for dysfunctional thoughts, individuals may be able to more quickly identify cognitive errors when they occur. More generally, patients are asked to treat their thoughts as hypotheses, and to ask themselves:

- What is the evidence for this thought?
- What is the evidence against this thought?

By evaluating the evidence, with sensitivity to common errors in reasoning (as provided below; see the appendix for a patient handout), patients can become adept at catching and starting to change their dysfunctional thinking habits.

The following clinician (C)/patient (P) dialogue, taken from *Managing Bipolar Disorder: A Cognitive-Behavioral Approach* (Otto et al., 2009), provides an example of

Table 3.1 Common Types of Negative Automatic Thoughts

Type of Thought	Sample Thought
All-or-Nothing Thinking	"I can't do anything right"
Catastrophizing	"It will be awful if I can't do it"
Discounting Positives	"I just got lucky"
Fortunetelling	"I won't do it right"
Labeling	"I'm an idiot"
Mind Reading	"They think I am stupid"
"Should" Statements	"I should be the best"

Adapted from Burns (1980)

the therapeutic use of the list of common cognitive errors with a patient with bipolar disorder:

> **C:** This is a list of some common distortions people make in their thinking when depressed. We are going to briefly review these types of thinking errors in order to give you some examples of the way in which depression may be influencing your thinking. OK?
>
> **P:** OK.
>
> **C:** One type of cognitive error is all-or-nothing thinking. This type of error, also known as black-and-white thinking, refers to seeing things as either completely good or completely bad, with no gray or middle ground. An example of this would involve a person viewing him- or herself as either a complete success or a complete failure. Unfortunately, life is often not so clear-cut, and very few individuals completely succeed or fail at everything. Most of life is in shades of gray. Can you think of any examples of how you might think in black-and-white terms?
>
> **P:** No. Not really.
>
> **C:** Well, how about earlier in today's session when you were saying that your life is worthless now that you have bipolar disorder?
>
> **P:** It does seem like everything is screwed up now.
>
> **C:** There, you have said it well for discussing black-and-white thinking. You said, "EVERYTHING is screwed up now." Can you think of any examples of things that may still be working OK?
>
> **P:** Well, my attention is on the things the bipolar disorder is affecting, but I guess my life isn't completely changed.
>
> **C:** Let's look at what things may still be working.
>
> **P:** Well, I guess I am still a good parent and my kids seem to care about me. I am changing jobs, but it seems like employers are still interested in me.
>
> **C:** Great. You just changed your extreme thinking to a more balanced view. With just a moment's thinking, you realized that saying "EVERYTHING is screwed up" is not true. I want you to remember this example as one way your thoughts may not be accurate. Instead of presenting a balanced view of your own circumstances, it may be easy, particularly when depressed, to over-focus on just a few of the facts. If you had to restate your unbalanced version of your life ("EVERYTHING is screwed up") in a more accurate fashion, what would you say?
>
> **P:** Well, some things are screwed up, but some things do seem to be working.
>
> **C:** That's it. The importance of catching all-or-nothing thinking is that it is much easier to live in a world where *some* things are screwed up and *some* things

are working, than to try to cope with a worldview that EVERYTHING is screwed up.

P: Yeah, it doesn't sound as bad.

COGNITIVE RESTRUCTURING FOR ANXIETY DISORDERS

Aside from teaching classic cognitive errors, there is benefit to teaching patients about the common types of distortions that occur in select disorders. For example, for the anxiety disorders, two distortions in thinking are common: (1) overestimation of the probability of negative outcomes, and (2) overestimation of the degree of catastrophe related to these outcomes. For example, in panic disorder, patients may overestimate the likelihood of negative outcomes linked to feared symptoms ("I will faint;" "I will have a heart attack;" "I will have to run out of the room") and/or the degree of catastrophe of these outcomes ("It will be horrible;" "I will never recover"). Accordingly, cognitive restructuring is frequently directed toward helping patients more accurately re-estimate the likelihood of feared outcomes (e.g., during how many panic attacks did you fear that you might faint, and then how frequently did you actually faint?) or to consider their actual coping abilities with negative outcomes. To achieve the latter goal, patients frequently need help going from global negative terms (e.g., "unbearable, horrible, terrible") to descriptions of what would actually occur ("I would get embarrassed") and whether this was a manageable event ("Have you ever been embarrassed before? How did you cope with those feelings?").

Overall, in helping patients treat thoughts as guesses about the world rather than statements of facts, clinicians will want to ensure that patients are adept at catching their cognitive errors. Additional ways clients can discover these errors/catastrophic expectations may include asking themselves such questions as:

- What's the worst that could happen? Would I live through it?
- What's the best that could happen?
- What's the most realistic outcome?
- What is the effect of my believing the automatic thought?
- What is the cognitive error?
- If a friend were in this situation and had this thought, what would I tell him or her?

THOUGHT MONITORING FOR DEPRESSION AND ANXIETY

As noted, a classic tool in teaching patients to monitor and react differently to dysfunctional thoughts is the Thought Record. This form is used to monitor, evaluate, and modify thoughts, with the goal of improving mood. The record consists of multiple columns used to separately document (a) the situation or event that triggered an unpleasant emotion, (b) the emotion triggered, (c) the associated automatic thought, (d) an evaluation of the accuracy of the automatic thought, and (e) the revised emotional response (after employing cognitive restructuring techniques). Review of Thought Records in session also forms the basis of active, cognitive restructuring rehearsal, where the clinician has the opportunity to provide direct feedback, or guided discovery, on the accuracy and usefulness of specific thoughts. A blank Thought Record is provided below. Patients are asked to complete entries daily, starting with review of mood changes and the events and thoughts surrounding them. Typically, in early sessions the clinician then evaluates the accuracy of the thoughts and introduces alternative conceptualizations. Later in treatment, the patient assumes these duties from the therapist. In this process, cognitive restructuring typically "marches backward in time" toward greater usefulness. In early applications, patients generate alternative thoughts and emotional responses hours after the event, but later in therapy, this restructuring occurs soon after the event, and then finally alternative responses to thoughts occur in real time in the situation. Regular and repeated practice of the process of cognitive restructuring aids this process, with overall guidance toward what "in-the-moment" cognitive restructuring might feel like with the use of conceptual metaphors, like the CEO metaphor provided earlier.

Thought Record

Situation (Describe the event that led to the unpleasant emotion)	Emotion (Specify sad, angry, etc., and rate the emotion from 0% to 100%)	Automatic Thought (Write the automatic thought and rate your belief in the thought from 0% to 100%)	Evaluation of Automatic Thought (Evaluate the accuracy of the automatic thought)	Re-rate Emotion (Re-rate the emotion and your belief in the thought from 0% to 100%)

The following discussion of the clinical introduction of a Thought Record between clinician and patient is adapted from Otto et al. (2009, Chapter 5):

C: The Thought Record will help you identify your negative thoughts, how you feel when you think these particular thoughts, how to evaluate them to see just how accurate they are, and then how to generate alternative thoughts.

P: That sounds like a tall order. I don't know what I'm thinking half the time.

C: We'll approach this in a step-by-step fashion. We'll focus first on identifying your dysfunctional thoughts and associated feelings. Once you get that, we'll focus on evaluating the accuracy of your thoughts and begin generating alternative ways of viewing events. Let's use an example to get you started. Do you remember when you came into session today and said you've been sad and frustrated since you talked with your mom on the phone this morning?

P: Yes, I really have been. It seems like I always get upset when I talk to my mom.

C: Well, I'd like you to try to think back to this morning and your phone conversation with her. Try to remember the point when you started to feel sad. Can you do that?

P: The conversation started and things went pretty well. Then she started asking me about my job search. She just doesn't seem to get it: I'm doing the best I can to find a job.

C: OK. When she asked you about the job search, do you recall what went through your mind or what you were thinking about?

P: I really don't know. But every time she asks me about my job situation it always upsets me.

C: That is a good observation. When we experience a change in mood or an intense emotion, we are often engaging in automatic thoughts that we are not likely aware of. So when your mom was asking you about the job search, it made you upset, right?

C: Yes.

(If patient has difficulty reporting thoughts, paradoxical questioning can be used to help elicit thoughts. For example, in the following statement, the therapist suggests a thought that is likely to be opposite to what the patient was actually thinking in the situation with her mother.)

C: So I bet you were having some thoughts when you began to feel upset or what you also called sad and frustrated. Maybe you were thinking about how proud your mom is that you are working so hard to find a job!

P: Yeah, right! She is not supportive at all. Actually, when she asked me about my job search, I was thinking that I'll never find a job and that I'm going to have to depend on my parents forever.

C: So you thought about your parents having to support you. What else?

P: Then I thought about what a loser I am because I don't have a job yet. And how successful all my friends are and how happy they are at their jobs. I thought about how pathetic my life is.

C: Well there you go. You came up with what you were thinking when you started to feel sad and frustrated. As I said before, when you notice a shift in your feelings you may be engaging in automatic thoughts that are not useful. Take notice and describe the feelings to yourself. Try to label them if possible. A helpful question to ask yourself is, "What is going through my mind right now?" Let's see if you can transfer this example onto the Thought Record.

P: So where do I write this?

T: I like to start with the second column, the feelings. First put down your feelings of sadness and frustration.

P: OK.

C: Now write out the thoughts that you told me. You said that you were having thoughts like, "I am a loser" and "My life is pathetic." What do you think of those thoughts now that you have them down in black and white?

P: Wow, they look pretty severe.

C: That is part of the value of writing out thoughts. It gives you a chance to see just how nasty you may talk to yourself at times. How do you think most people would feel when faced by thoughts of this kind?

P: I would imagine they would feel like hell, but what's the alternative? Do you want me to go around all the time thinking, "Oh, my life is so good"? I really wonder sometimes whether I will have a good life or whether I am a loser.

C: Let's take a moment and consider that question. You are in a position right now where you are rather freely using the term "loser" to describe yourself, apparently because you haven't yet found a job. If you're going to use a term like that, you'd better define it for me. What is a loser?

P: I don't know. I guess a loser is a person, you know, who never does anything worthwhile, never achieves anything.

C: And how true is that for you, that you never do anything worthwhile?

P: Well, I don't have a job.

C: That wasn't what I asked. I know you don't have a job right now, but is it true that you never do anything worthwhile?

P: (laughing) No. I actually do a number of things right, and to tell the truth I got one job offer, it was just that the job was lousy.

C: OK, so you are telling me, that according to your definition, you do not meet criteria for a loser?

P: Right, but sometimes I feel like a loser.

C: Ahhh, that is an important distinction. You know logically that you are not a loser, but at times you FEEL like a loser.

P: Yeah.

C: And can you think of any reasons why your FEELINGS about yourself may be especially negative?

P: So you think this is part of the depression.

C: Yes, I do think that you are primed right now to FEEL like lots of things are not going well. That is part of depression. And, because you are depressed, I want you to be especially careful about buying into these feelings and coaching yourself with words like LOSER.

P: It can't be good for my depression, can it?

C: No, it can't. Thinking about it now, what might be a more accurate way of coaching yourself around not having a job?

P: Well, I might say, this feels like hell, but I did get one offer. But isn't this just thinking "happy thoughts"?

C: No, it is more like thinking accurate thoughts. Thinking happy thoughts would be more like, "It is a bright cheery day, and I will get a job today for sure."

P: (laughs)

C: I'm not trying to get you to think happy thoughts; instead, I'm trying to help your thoughts serve you by being accurate. I want your thoughts to be useful for you, and I know calling yourself a loser just does not help, especially when you are depressed. Remember, it is important that you act as a therapist for yourself, to guide yourself with your thoughts.

P: To be a better coach of myself in my head.

C: Exactly. And now that you had a chance to evaluate your thoughts, what is your mood when you think about not having a job?

P: Well it isn't good, but at least I don't feel like dirt.

C: This is a good start. Now let's talk about how you can apply what we talked about in home practice.

Figure 3.1 shows what the Thought Record for the patient in the preceding case example would look like.

THERAPEUTIC STYLE AND
COGNITIVE RESTRUCTURING

It is important for clinicians to adapt a therapeutic style that provides a comfortable emotional fit with the patient. The term "comfortable fit" is hard to describe but in part describes a collaborative and emotionally rich effort that keeps as its focus the patient's best interests. As we have argued elsewhere (Otto et al., 2009), a well-toned "hmmm" can replace a full question, or the exclamation "Ouch!" can be used to replace the

Situation	Emotion	Automatic thought	Evaluation of automatic thought	Re-rate emotion
(Describe the event that led to the unpleasant emotion)	(Specify sad, angry, etc., and rate the emotion from 0% to 100%)	(Write the automatic thought and rate your belief in the thought from 0% to 100%)	(Evaluate the accuracy of the automatic thought)	(Re-rate the emotion and your belief in the thought from 0% to 100%)
Spoke to my mom on the phone. She asked me about my job search.	Sad 90% Frustrated 95%	I will never find a job and will have to rely on my parents forever. I am a loser. Belief in thoughts = 95%	I actually did get one job offer, but it wasn't right for me. Even though I may feel like a loser, I have experienced success in my life.	Sad 25% Frustrated 40%

Figure 3.1 Sample Thought Record

phrase, "That sounds like a rather harsh self-criticism." Indeed, some of the luminaries of CBT are famous, in part, for the way in which they bring their personalities to the task of effective cognitive restructuring. Dr. A. T. Beck, for example, is known for the tremendous interpersonal warmth he brings to the task of Socratic questioning. Although the questioning may be straightforward ("Can you think of any alternative explanations for what may have been going on with that event?"), it is done with such warmth and curiosity that the experience of the self-discovery of dysfunctional thoughts and their alternative is both a palpable and pleasurable process for the patient.

A different kind of memorable experience was provided in the cognitive restructur-ing of Dr. Albert Ellis. Ellis, famous for his curmudgeon-like approach to cognitive restructuring, could provide a compelling, emotional, and memorable way for patients to restructure their thoughts. Ellis, while conveying warmth and respect for the patient, could display a caustic disrespect for dysfunctional thoughts, and thereby aid the patient in rapid adoption of an alternative cognitive style.

Whereas each of these approaches were appropriate to the personal style of the luminaries in the field that practiced them, it is up to each individual clinician to develop a style that rapidly and effectively communicates to patients that (1) thoughts can have powerful effects on emotion and motivation, (2) these effects can occur regardless of whether the thoughts are accurate or not, (3) it is common to have inaccurate and dysfunctional thoughts, especially in the mood and anxiety disorders, (4) thoughts should not be taken at face value, and (5) a mindful approach to evaluating thoughts (and for not taking them too seriously) can have powerful beneficial effects on mood and anxiety disorders.

In addition to having clinicians consider the range of interpersonal styles that can be used to achieve these goals for cognitive restructuring, we would also like clinicians to consider the value of storytelling to achieve these aims. The following story (adapted originally from Otto, 2000; see Otto et al., 2009) can be used to provide initial training in the evaluation of thoughts and the adoption of more adaptive self-talk. The goal of using storytelling is to provide a compelling and memorable event to help guide a patient toward behavior change. Storytelling is aided by the effective use of changes in vocal tone and tempo, as well as theatrical pauses and gestures. The goal is to make the story memorable for later use by patients:

This is a story about Little League baseball. I talk about Little League baseball because of the amazing parents and coaches involved. And by "amazing" I don't mean good. I mean extreme.

But this story doesn't start with the coaches or the parents; it starts with Johnny, who is a Little League player in the outfield. His job is to catch fly balls and return them to the infield players. On the day of our story, Johnny is in the outfield and crack!—one of the players on the other team hits a fly ball. The ball is coming to Johnny. Johnny raises his glove. The ball is coming to him, coming to him . . . . . . and it goes over his head. Johnny misses the ball, and the other team scores a run.

Now there are a number of ways a coach can respond to this situation. Let's take Coach A first. Coach A is the type of coach who will come out on the field and shout: "I can't believe you missed that ball! Anyone could have caught it! My dog could have caught it! You screw up like that again and you'll be sitting on the bench! That was lousy!" Coach A then storms off the field.

At this point, Johnny is standing in the outfield and, if he is at all similar to me, he is tense, tight, trying not to cry, and praying that another ball is not hit to him. If a ball does come to him, Johnny will probably miss it. After all, he is tense and tight and may see four balls coming at him because of the tears in his eyes. If we are Johnny's parents, we may see more profound changes after the game. Johnny, who typically places his baseball glove on the mantel, now throws it under his bed. And before the next game, he may complain that his stomach hurts, that perhaps he should not go to the game. This is the scenario with Coach A.

Now let's go back to the original event and play it differently. Johnny has just missed the ball, and now Coach B comes out on the field. Coach B says: "Well, you missed that one. Here is what I want you to remember: high balls look like they are farther away than they really are. Also, it is much easier to run forward than to back up. Because of this, I want you to prepare for the ball by taking a few extra steps backwards. As the ball gets closer you can step into it if you need to. Also, try to catch it at chest level, so you can adjust your hand if you misjudge the ball. Let's see how you do next time." Coach B then leaves the field.

How does Johnny feel? Well, he is not happy—after all, he missed the ball—but there are a number of important differences from the way he felt with Coach A. He is not as tense or tight, and if a fly ball does come to him, he knows what to do differently to catch it. And because he does not have tears in his eyes, he may actually see the ball and catch it.

So, if we were the type of parent who wanted Johnny to make the Major Leagues, we would pick Coach B, because he teaches Johnny how to be a more effective player. Johnny knows what to do differently, may catch more balls, and may grow to excel at the game.

But if we didn't care whether Johnny made the Major Leagues—because baseball is a game, and one is supposed to be able to enjoy a game—then we would again pick Coach B. We would pick Coach B because we care whether Johnny enjoys the game. With Coach B, Johnny knows what to do differently; he is not tight, tense, and ready to cry; he may catch a few balls; and he may enjoy the game. He may also continue to place his glove on the mantel.

Now, while we may all select Coach B for Johnny, we rarely choose the voice of Coach B for the way we talk to ourselves. Think about your last mistake. Did you say, "I can't believe I did that! I am so stupid! What a jerk!"? These are "Coach A" thoughts, and they have many of the same effects on us as Coach A has on Johnny. These thoughts make us feel tense and tight, may make us feel like crying, and rarely help us do better in the future. Remember, even if you were only concerned about productivity (making the Major League), you would still pick Coach B. And if you were concerned with enjoying life, with guiding yourself effectively for both joy and productivity, you certainly would pick Coach B.

During the next week, I would like you to listen to see how you are coaching yourself. If you hear Coach A, remember this story and see if you can replace "Coach A" thoughts with "Coach B" thoughts.

One therapeutic strategy is to close a session with the coaching story, to make the story the most salient feature of the session and to capitalize on recency effects (enhanced memory for the most recent event). The goal is to maximize the patient's memory cues for the story so that cognitive restructuring during the week will naturally occur in relation to the core message of the story. Also, as with any intervention, it is important for the clinician to reinstate memories of the intervention for the patient in the next session. For example, clinicians may say:

Last week, I presented you with a story about coaching styles. Tell me what you thought of the story and what you noticed about your own style of self-talk during the past week. Did you tend to talk to yourself like Coach A or Coach B?

If necessary, clinicians may want to reiterate relevant parts from the story, asking the patient about his or her experience with the different coaching styles, with specific encouragement of adoption of a "Coach B" style.

PROMOTING ADAPTIVE COGNITIVE CHANGE

No matter what style is chosen for cognitive restructuring interventions, in almost every session, we would like clinicians to attend to helping patients shift the way in which they view their own thoughts. This should occur regardless of the disorder being treated. As a matter of course in therapy, we want patients to learn to more dispassionately process their own thoughts, to view them as behaviors that may or may not be useful, to know that thoughts can have a powerful effect on emotions regardless of their accuracy, and to put some effort into developing an alternative cognitive style. We believe that a more mindful cognitive style (CEO thinking) is a core skill that can be applied to any of the disorder-based interventions described in the later chapters. We also believe that you, the reader/clinician, should rehearse this style for yourself, observing your own personal coaching strategies, and then using the knowledge you gain to help you select a cognitive restructuring style for your patients that can be delivered in a compelling and memorable way. Regardless of whether you tell stories, offer up warm Socratic questioning, or jokingly challenge specific dysfunctional thoughts, it is up to you to translate the cognitive interventions exemplified in the disorder-specific chapters into a style that can be accepted and productively used by your patients. Cognitive restructuring need never be a sterile or overly cerebral activity. Instead, it should be a rich and memorable strategy for helping patients change some of the core processes that maintain disorders.

4

ACTIVITY AND EXPOSURE ASSIGNMENTS

One of the ways in which CBT differs from other psychosocial treatments is in its direct programming of change through activity and exposure assignments. These assignments help ensure that treatment is not over-focused on thinking rather than doing, and also reflect an emphasis on the importance of experience in changing both cognitions and affect. In short, people learn by doing, and CBT utilizes successive practices in the session and in the patient's everyday life to help the patient acquire and become comfortable with new ways of being.

For mood and anxiety disorders, activity interventions target a return to productive and joyful activities. This represents a dismantling of one of the core affective messages of depression—to pull in and conserve resources ("don't try," "it won't work," "there is no point")—while ensuring that patients are exposed to the events in life that boost and maintain mood. Typically these involve achievement-related activities (including completing small home or work tasks) as well as pleasurable activities (a movie out, playing cards with friends, etc.), and, increasingly, exercise. For the anxiety disorders, exposure interventions involve a step-by-step relearning of safety and comfort in relation to feared cues. These cues prominently include people, places, and things, but also include the internal environment, including the experience of anxiety itself. In other words, behavioral treatment involves an active undoing of maladaptive and affect-driven responses. Patients learn to pursue meaningful mood and life goals, regardless of their emotional urge at the moment. Investing emotional discomfort in the short term allows patients to achieve more pleasant emotional experiences in the long term. For depression, it is developing the ability to plan, choose, and execute pleasant activities without "feeling like it." For anxiety disorders, it is the ability to tolerate the peaks of anxiety that occur when first re-confronting a feared situation or event in order to enjoy the reductions in this anxiety as one persists in these situations. Accordingly, behavioral activity or exposure assignments routinely provide patients some implicit training with emotional tolerance; patients learn not to wait for a congruent mood state (a good mood or low anxiety) before pursuing valued activities. Because of this feature, we will open our discussion of activity and exposure assignments with examples of how patients learn to react differently to their own emotional experience, both in CBT and in therapy more generally.

EMOTIONAL ACCEPTANCE AND TOLERANCE

We believe effective therapy always involves emotional exposure of some sort. This is because talking about painful life experiences (as one does in therapy) forces us to tolerate the emotions evoked by the memory of the experience. Hence, to adequately discuss these episodes in treatment (psychopharmacologic or psychosocial), a person has to be able to tolerate the emotions evoked by the discussion. Greater comfort with these evoked emotions means greater comfort in therapy.

Across different orientations to therapy, attention is regularly devoted (implicitly or explicitly) to enhancing comfort with these feelings. When we see a patient become embarrassed about crying in session, we lean forward and offer comfort and acceptance of that emotion, giving the message either tacitly or expressly that "it is OK to have emotions in therapy." This is emotional acceptance in its most rudimentary form: by our responses to a patient's emotion, we teach that emotional acceptance is a value. And if we do not do this, we can be a force in helping patients *avoid emotion*, by either avoiding talking about emotional topics or avoiding treatment sessions altogether. The result is slower and ultimately less effective therapy.

Accordingly, we believe that comfort with one's own emotional experience is a rate-limiting step (emotional discomfort can slow therapy) in most psychosocial treatments. Issues of comfort with emotional experiences are also characteristic of several disorders. For example, both panic disorder and posttraumatic stress disorder (PTSD) are characterized by high fears of anxiety and related sensations (anxiety sensitivity), and modification of these fears of anxiety is at the core of CBT for panic disorder. Fears of these symptoms are also linked to a wide variety of other maladaptive emotional coping patterns, including the use of tobacco, alcohol, or food to cope with stress (see Academic Moment, Box 4.1), and corrective interventions (once specific to panic disorder) are being applied more frequently across disorders. This process has been most formalized in CBT for panic disorder, where patients are systematically exposed to anxiety-like sensations (e.g., through hyperventilation to produce feelings of lightheadedness, numbness and tingling, flushing, and feelings of unreality) and have the opportunity to learn comfort with these sensations, in part by noticing the induced sensations while doing nothing to manage them. Preparation for this *interoceptive exposure* involves cognitive restructuring—helping patients identify and begin to change their catastrophic misinterpretation of these sensations (e.g., "I am having a stroke," "I am losing control," "I will faint and will embarrass myself"). Also, at least minimal cognitive restructuring is applied after exposure to help patients maximize their learning from specific exposure practice. This may involve having patients state what they conclude from the exposure, and how they want to use that information to guide themselves when they next encounter the phobic stimulus (in this case, anxiety sensations). In short, well-planned exposure procedures include the preparation of a cognitive "landing zone" for the experiences to be induced, providing a way for patients to think about and begin to experience their feelings of anxious discomfort in a new way. Chapter 6 provides some explicit training in these methods as applied to panic disorder.

Box 4.1 Academic Moment: Fears and Intolerance of Anxiety-Like Sensations

Interoceptive exposure emerged in the 1980s as a treatment for panic disorder. An early report by Grieze and van den Hout (1983) described CO_2 inhalation to induce feared bodily sensations during the first week of intensive exposure, followed by three weeks of situational exposure for the treatment of panic attacks. Much more easy-to-arrange strategies (e.g., running stairs, hyperventilation, straw-breathing, or spinning in a chair) surfaced over time, and comprehensive CBT programs using these treatments have been especially effective (Gould, Otto & Pollack, 1995). Anxiety sensitivity itself was conceptualized as a fundamental fear that may underlie other phobic conditions (see McNally, 2002) that is, individuals may fear a range of stimuli—enclosed places, heights, snakes—because of fears of the induced feelings of anxiety (e.g., "I can't stand the way I feel when I am in an enclosed space"). Accordingly, anxiety sensitivity can be thought of as an amplifying factor, amplifying the aversiveness of anxiety-like sensations and motivating (maladaptive) avoidance or escape responses. This concept has proven valuable across a range of disorders. In addition to identifying people at risk for the emergence of panic disorder or panic attacks following stress (Gardenswartz & Craske, 2001; Schmidt, Lerew & Jackson, 1997) and predicting recurrent panic attacks (e.g., Ehlers, 1995), it has been found useful for predicting dyspnea-related distress and avoidance in individuals with pulmonary disease (COPD; Carr, Lehrer & Hochron, 1995; Simon et al., 2006), level of pain complaints (Ocanez et al., 2010), risk for failure in smoking cessation attempts (e.g., Brown, Kahler, Zvolensky,

Lejuez & Ramsey, 2001), and dropout in residential treatment programs for substance dependence (Lejuez et al., 2008). With documentation of the role of anxiety sensitivity in all of these conditions, there have been corresponding investigations of the treatment, with interoceptive exposure strategies, of these fears and the maladaptive avoidance responses that accompany them (see Otto, 2008).

More generally, though, we advise preparing patients to have a plan for how they react to their emotional experience as they engage in activity assignments or exposure therapy. As discussed in the previous chapter, we recommend a mindful (or marveling) approach: having patients actively note, label, and then marvel at their emotional content (and the behavioral urges to escape or avoid in response to these emotions), while taking time to decide what the adaptive action is, independent of this emotional signal. As one may guess, the CEO approach (Chapter 3) can be very useful with this process: it helps patients to be aware of their emotion as just one part of the "company" of inputs to which they need to attend. Then, with empathy, they decide which actions are most appropriate for the well-being of the company, independent of this emotional voice.

In this process, it is important to stress appropriate kindness and empathy for the emotion by the patient (as well as by the clinician). Activity assignments and exposure therapy sessions are never meant to be exercises in stoicism. Instead, we want patients to respond to their own emotional experience with empathy, awareness, and kindness. In terms of an internal dialogue, patients may say:

> *Ouch, I hurt (am anxious, lonely, sad, etc.). Given this feeling, what do I have the urge to do? And given what I know about my disorder, what might be best for me to do to help myself?*

Many patients with anxiety and mood disorders will already have a strong repertoire of self-empathy that can be used as part of this process. At other times, however, this empathic voice may be lost, sometimes due to the chronicity of a disorder or because this kind self-coaching response was never learned during development. For example, we believe that one reason why therapy is so challenging for patients with borderline personality disorder is because these patients are missing the ability to provide self-comfort. Those with borderline personality disorder often possess a cruel, self-critical cognitive style that leads them to lash out, deny, or otherwise avoid or escape their own emotional experiences. Moreover, at the individual moments of emotional pain, there seems to be no agency for self-help: to ask, "What have I learned in therapy that may be of value at this moment?" Without this moment-by-moment application of helpful strategies, therapy will take substantially longer. Likewise, with chronic depression, patients may learn to respond to a sad mood with fear and self-criticism, "Oh, no, I better not be feeling depressed again. What is wrong with me?" At other times, these types of ruminative patterns may dominate such that it is difficult for patients to initiate other patterns. For these moments, we have applied explicit training on how to react to one's own emotional experience.

One prominent example of this training comes from our approach to the treatment of PTSD in Cambodian survivors of the Pol Pot-era genocide. As part of interventions for this non–English-speaking refugee population, we had to devise treatment elements for PTSD that could be communicated clearly and rapidly through a translator (Otto & Hinton, 2006). In other words, our communication with patients had to be both brief and efficient. We needed to use discrete "sound bites" of information that did not overwhelm the interpreters with content and that would be clear as a single unit of information. This was especially important because with the time of translation—each unit of information had to be translated, discussed, and back-translated to the clinician—any poorly presented concept that led to off-track discussions would waste valuable minutes of therapeutic time. Accordingly, we sought to deliver as many core therapeutic concepts in terms of metaphors that either operated across cultures or were already well known within the Cambodian culture.

One such concept was used to describe how to manage the emotion brought from exposure to a trauma cue. Patients were already instructed in ways to understand the source of their fears in terms of a past event, and soothe themselves while discriminating past fears from the current situation. We added instruction in emotional acceptance to this process. To explain this concept, we borrowed the notion of "three bows." Within our patients' culture, when one enters a temple, one bows three times, with reverence, to the statue of the Buddha. We adopted these three bows of reverence to introduce a non-ruminative cognitive response to follow the processing of trauma-cue exposures:

1. The first bow was a deep and personal acknowledgement that the trauma was severe: "It was bad, and it hurt me."
2. The second bow was an acknowledgment that the trauma has had enduring effects: "It hurt me then, and it hurt me over time."
3. The third bow was an acknowledgment of a desire for change in the present: "I am here now and I want a better life."

Just as they used three bows to respect the Buddha, Cambodian refugee patients were taught to use these three thoughts (with pauses in between) to convey their respect for the enormity of the experience they survived during the Pol Pot years and after, and to provide themselves with an emotionally meaningful but non-ruminative response to their exposure experiences.

This method for promoting emotional acceptance is just one example of preparing a coping plan for patients to use when asking them to engage in new behaviors in response to old emotional cues. A detailed metaphor may not be needed, but we do recommend that clinicians help prepare their patients for exposure and activity assignments by asking the following:

> *What thoughts are you going to have before you start the assignment, and what thoughts might you have that may sap your enthusiasm either before or during the assignment?*
>
> *What emotions are you going to feel during the assignment, and how do you want to talk to yourself about these feelings?*

EXPOSURE ASSIGNMENTS

In arranging exposure therapy for anxiety patients, clinicians have three central tasks: (1) helping the patient identify the core fears underlying the anxiety disorder, (2) designing exposure interventions wherein the patient is able to safely confront and cope with the feared cues, and (3) helping patients cope with fears in a variety of different circumstances so patients realize they are able to cope in real life in the future. In the disorder-specific chapters that follow, we provide information on the core patterns (supported by psychopathology studies) that underlie each disorder, and indicate the core fears to be targeted by exposure interventions, where relevant. However, these chapters do not adequately convey the philosophy of arranging exposure interventions, and consideration of the additive nature of the various elements of patients' phobic experience.

Chapter 3 already reviewed the use of Socratic questions ("Help me understand exactly why that is bothersome; what about being embarrassed seems so bad?") to help patients move from global negative statements ("It will be horrible") or general statements about negative outcomes ("I might faint") to specific concerns ("If I faint I will get embarrassed; if people see me they may call me an idiot"). Answers to these questions will help inform the clinician about the elements of the phobic situation that may be important for inclusion in the exposure experience. For example, if the concern about dizziness is linked to concerns about being embarrassed in front of others, then the induction of dizziness (via hyperventilation) may need to be done, ultimately, in the context of standing and performing a social task while dizzy. The key question for the clinician is what needs to be learned from an exposure experience to provide the patient with a sense of safety with respect to the phobic concern. In addressing this question, we want the clinician to use an additive model of the core phobic concern.

For example, for a patient with panic disorder who is phobic about driving, the clinician needs to determine the particular elements of the patient's experience that cue anxiety. For example, the fear of driving on the expressway while panicking can be broken into the following elements:

- in the car
- driving on the expressway
- busy traffic
- no exits available
- being alone in the car
- thinking "I can't make it; I am going to crash the car"
- experiencing panic symptoms (dizzy, flushed, heart racing, breathless)

The clinician should arrange the stepwise exposure to each of these elements alone or in combination in order for the patient to learn to be comfortable with the fear cues. How high the clinician wants to start in the fear hierarchy (see staging of exposure below) determines the sequence of combination necessary to help ensure stepwise success. Traditionally, for panic disorder we start with interoceptive exposure to anxiety sensations conducted in the office. For this patient, this will include preparation in terms of providing a model of panic disorder and orienting patients to the role and (anxiogenic) function of catastrophic thinking patterns. After preparatory planning for thinking alternatively about these symptoms, the clinician would introduce interoceptive exposure (e.g., induction of dizziness, racing heart, or shortness of breath) while the patient is with him or her in the office. Once the patient learns initial comfort with these sensations (in part by attending to them, doing nothing to control them, and relaxing in the presence of the sensations; see Chapter 6), then the clinician can proceed to assign home induction of these sensations as part of interoceptive exposure. With home assignment, the clinician has provided the first additive step.

1. **Panic Sensations in the Office**
2. **Panic Sensations + Alone**

Once the patient returns and reports comfort with this assignment, the clinician can start chaining together additional phobic cues. For example, the clinician may introduce some of the traditional catastrophic thoughts to help the patient become inured to these habitual thoughts while experiencing panic sensations. Indeed, for some patients, this exposure to thoughts becomes a more formal process, with the clinician asking the patient to repeat the catastrophic thought aloud 20 times. Across this repetition, most patients report that the salience of the thought has changed and has become less frightening. Home practice would then include exposure to this thought when not anxious, and, finally, to include the thought in the context of interoceptive exposure to provide:

3. Panic Sensations + Alone + Intentional Catastrophic Thoughts

In-session exposure exercises could then include having the patient imagine being in the car and feeling the anxiety symptoms. Home practice could include having the patient practice exposure by sitting in a parked car.

4. Panic Sensations + Alone + Thoughts + Sitting in Car

Driving the car after symptom induction (with rehearsal of appropriate driving skills of attending to the road; see Academic Moment box below) would then follow to provide:

5. Panic Sensations + Alone + Thoughts + Car + Driving

Depending on the patient's level of fear, exposure practice can include driving different routes or driving at heavy traffic times. When enough relevant cues have been included in the exposure (safety learning), the patient is ready to drive on the expressway. At this point, the patient has become comfortable with panic sensations, so it is unlikely that he or she will have a panic attack during the exposure. Even if the patient does experience panic, he or she should be able to manage the symptoms, effectively ending the fear cycle that maintains the disorder (see Chapter 6).

Box 4.2 Academic Moment: Learning to Be Effective While Anxious

There are two types of learning that are operative during driving exposures. One is the learning of safety in the context of fear cues (less anxious arousal while driving), but the other is the rehearsal of effective driving skills in the context of anxiety (better driving while having anxious arousal). The latter learning is important for patients with driving phobias (e.g., panic with agoraphobia that includes driving fears) who tend to freeze up, become inattentive, brake excessively, or switch lanes erratically when anxious. These patients need rehearsal of better driving skills while anxious. This rehearsal also takes place during exposure practice but may need to be reviewed during the session (and in fuller CBT may be rehearsed if the clinician chooses to accompany the patient during the driving exposure). To illustrate this type of learning, a metaphor is apt. Think of old newsreel presentations of soldiers

---

undergoing basic training during World War II. One such newsreel shows soldiers crawling through the mud under barbed wire while live machine gun rounds are fired over their heads. The narrator intones that the soldiers are learning not to be afraid under such conditions. Wrong! These soldiers are certainly afraid of live rounds whizzing over their heads, and they *should* be afraid. They are not learning to be unafraid. They are learning to perform well under conditions of such fear: to crawl forward, keep their heads low, and fire their rifles on command. These are the necessary skills of a combat soldier, and learning not to freeze up in response to fear is crucial. Likewise, interoceptive exposure helps train patients to *keep their heads* during fear, and this skill needs to be extended to the driving situation. By learning to relax with sensations of fear and to focus on relevant behaviors (e.g., maintaining speed, checking mirrors before changing lanes), patients can learn to be safer drivers with effective exposure. A broader point is also relevant here. When individuals learn to be more comfortable with their experience of anxiety, *everything* can become easier. If anxiety becomes a less aversive signal—during meetings with a boss, conflict situations, spousal arguments— patients (and clinicians alike) can better keep their heads when anxious. Interoceptive exposure is a valuable tool for such learning.

To review, in arranging exposure interventions, clinicians need to be attentive to arranging exposure experiences that most directly lead to the learning of true safety. To achieve this end, clinicians need to understand the range of elements of the patient's core fears, and to provide exposure-based training in becoming comfortable with these elements. This may be done initially by working with discrete elements of the fear, but over time these elements should be combined so that the distinction between what is practiced for exposure in and out of session is no longer distinct from the array of cues that defines the patient's core fears. This chaining together of feared cues enables the clinician to target the most durable and relevant learning for the anxiety disorder. In the case of social anxiety disorder, for example, it is easy to focus on the patient's development of a sense of safety around a *well-done* social performance. However, a fuller acquisition of safety may require this to occur under *poor*-performance conditions, helping patients undo the true core fear of the consequences of everyday social errors. This would be accomplished by having patients actually practice difficult social exposures (e.g., spilling coffee in front of a group of co-workers) (see Chapter 9), which should lead to fuller safety learning than a focus on adequate-performance exposures alone.

SAFETY BEHAVIORS

Part of the cues and context that need to be considered when designing exposures is the presence of "safety behaviors." Safety behaviors refer to the subtle avoidance behaviors people apply to try to reduce the perceived threat of a phobic situation. In the case of social anxiety disorder, safety behaviors include such things as averting one's eyes while speaking in a social situation; in the case of panic disorder, safety behaviors may include carrying a cell phone or water bottle, or sedative medication such as a benzodiazepine. It appears that safety learning under conditions of a safety behavior is conditional: people learn that they are safe as long as they believe they can engage in their safety behavior, but the core fear may stay alive, putting patients at risk for incomplete response or relapse.

Box 4.3 Academic Moment: Safety Behaviors

As has been argued elsewhere (Powers et al., 2010), the defining characteristic of safety behaviors is not their form, but their function. Safety behaviors modify the perceived threat of a situation or event, even if the safety behavior does not have a logical link to outcomes. Research also suggests that safety behavior availability (in addition to actual use) may prevent the learning of unambiguous rather than conditional safety (i.e., "I am safe as long as I have my water bottle and cell phone handy"). Powers et al. (2004) showed that participants who had safety behaviors available during exposure treatment reported significantly *less* improvement compared to participants who did not rely on safety behaviors (response rates were 45% vs. 95%, respectively). These deleterious effects of safety behaviors were evident *whether patients used them or not*—indicating that the mere availability of safety behaviors can interfere with lasting fear reduction from exposure. Reducing the use of safety behaviors (e.g., stopping carrying a rescue pill of benzodiazepine medication) is accordingly important as exposure treatment progresses.

REACQUIRING PLEASURE DURING EXPOSURE

The goal of exposure is not to "tough it out," but to actively relearn a sense of safety in feared situations. This learning appears to be aided by full involvement in normal behavior during the exposure. What is normal? Normal in part includes having a goal for the exposure other than simply completing it. For example, if exposure includes going to the mall, then the exposure goal should also include shopping for a desired object. This helps patients persist in the phobic situation, with the overall goal of having a patient stay in a fear situation at least two to three times as long as it takes to become comfortable in that situation. In other words, if the patient takes 15 minutes to start to feel comfortable, it would be optimal (though sometimes not practical) to have the patient shop for at least an additional half-hour in that situation. Also, clinicians should attend to removing other phobic behaviors in the situation. This includes either under- or over-attending to the phobic stimulus. For example, a patient should explicitly try *not* to focus on the fact that the exit of the mall is no longer visible when he is in its center, but *should* try to notice that though he is far from the exit, he is near a store where he wants to shop and there are items in the store's window that interest him. This is normal mall behavior—looking around and window shopping—and hence is a relevant target during the exposure.

The materials provided here will help guide you in planning exposures for your clients. Table 4.1 provides an overview of exposure instruction, and the Exposure Planning Checklist on page 39 (also provided as a patient handout in the appendix) will help you plan exposures that take into account some of the additive cues and contexts that can affect the level of threat of a phobic situation. Both are reprinted from Powers et al., 2010.

Table 4.1 Constructing a Program of Exposure

1. Construct a model of the top-of-the-hierarchy fear for the patient using an additive model. In constructing the model, consider the range of additive cues that are part of the core fear, including external as well as internal environments (including feeling states, thoughts, and actions taken by the patient). Select the most relevant exposure exercises (e.g., interoceptive exposure for panic disorder or social exposures for social anxiety disorder), but then create a hierarchy of exposures by varying the additive cues present in the exposures.

2. Conduct the exposures while evaluating the safety learned by the patient. Elicitation of anxiety at exposure onset is a useful measure of a good match between the cues and the fear (indicating a relevant exposure), but good anxiety reduction across the exposure and evidence that feared outcomes did not occur (or were not as aversive as assumed) is the goal of the exposure practice.

3. Continue conducting the exposures with an eye toward varying the contexts of the exposure to ensure that the learning of safety is not conditional on a specific context. Make sure to vary the pre-comfort of the patient when going into exposures (idiosyncratic definitions of good vs. bad days, such as the presence of fatigue or anticipatory anxiety), the presence of the clinician or significant others, and the presence of other safety cues and behaviors. Use the Exposure Planning Checklist (above) to aid in the assessment of these cues.

Adapted from Powers, M. B., Vervliet, B., Smits, J. A. J., & Otto, M. W. (2010). Helping exposure succeed: Learning theory perspectives on treatment resistance and relapse. In M. W. Otto & S. G. Hofmann (Eds.), *Avoiding Treatment Failures in the Anxiety Disorders* (pp. 31–49). New York: Springer. With kind permission of Springer Science+Business Media.

Exposure Planning Checklist

Attending to the Correct Core Fear

What is/are the core fear or fears that should be targeted by treatment? Ask the patient:
"What is so bad about. . .." to elucidate the central feared features.

_____

_____

_____

Attending to the Contexts Surrounding the Fear

Aggravating Contexts

What are the contexts in which this fear is worse? Consider the following:

- Time of day/year (including light dark, certain weather conditions [e.g., hot weather
  in the case of panic disorder]): _____
- Presence of others (known or unknown people): _____
- Presence of symptoms (e.g., muscle tension, certain worries): _____
- Mental or physical fatigue (also including menstrual cycle): _____
- Interpersonal conflict: _____
- Other: _____
- Other: _____

Safety Behaviors/Events

What are the behaviors or events that lead the patient to assume relative safety from the
feared outcomes?

- Contact with others (e.g., cell phone, presence of safe other, knowledge of availability
  of safe other): _____
- Food or drink (bottle of water, mints, antacids, crackers, fruit):

  _____
- Something to hold (glass)/position near a wall or door:

  _____
- Medication (often benzodiazepine or beta-blocker use):

  _____
- Cognitive rituals (e.g., affirmations, lucky sayings):

  _____
- Body positions/eye contact (averting one's eyes while speaking,
  clasping the hands, leaning against a wall, bracing against a chair):

  _____
- Talking with others: _____
- Other: _____
- Other: _____
- Other: _____

Reprinted from Powers, M. B., Vervliet, B., Smits, J. A. J., & Otto, M. W. (2010). Helping exposure succeed: Learning theory perspectives on treatment resistance and relapse. In M. W. Otto & S. G. Hofmann
(Eds.), *Avoiding Treatment Failures in the Anxiety Disorders* (pp. 31–49). New York: Springer. With kind
permission of Springer Science+Business Media.

ACTIVITY ASSIGNMENTS

Exposure assignments for anxiety disorders have, as their end result, an activity assignment component: patients are to explicitly re-enter avoided situations and target normal (and ultimately pleasurable) behavior when in these situations. Activity assignments are used in the treatment of depression as well as anxiety. Depression brings with it pessimism, low motivation, and inactivity. As mood worsens, depression is characterized by negative memories, negative expectations, and further deteriorations in motivation. The result is that many depressed individuals become insulated from positive activities that could act as a natural antidepressant. Activity assignments are used to provide stepwise re-engagement in pleasant and meaningful events that can act as a buffer against feelings of depression, and provide an antidote to the patterns of inactivity and avoidance that characterize depression.

A first step in behavioral activation treatments is the identification of patterns of activity, inactivity, and avoidance in the patient's schedule. This is frequently done using a self-monitoring form (see the Weekly Activity Schedule in the Appendix of Forms and Handouts) with review of the form in a follow-up visit one week later. These completed forms can be strikingly informative. Some will reveal patterns of over-activity, with endless aversive tasks awaiting the patient on an hourly basis. Others will reveal severe under-activity and depression-related avoidance (e.g., staying in bed, skipping housework, not following through with responsibilities or social opportunities) and few opportunities for pleasant events.

The task of the clinician is to help the patient re-plan and schedule two classes of activities: achievement activities and pleasant events. Achievement activities are aimed at helping patients undo patterns of avoidance and eliciting the positive feelings that come from productive activity. Some of these productive activities may require multiple steps for achievement. Indeed, clinicians need to be vigilant to patterns of overenthusiastic goal setting, where patients have the wish to undo depressive patterns in one dramatic step (and thereby set themselves up for likely failure). The Steps to Goal Attainment form (see Appendix of Forms and Handouts) is designed to help patients examine the stepwise actions that can take them to their ultimate goals. Each week, patients are to schedule and monitor progress toward each step of these sequential goals.

In all cases, the starting point for achievement and pleasant event scheduling should be a level just higher than what is currently observed. In other words, the starting point on activity assignments is where the patient is currently, not where the patient wishes he or she is. Regular monitoring of progress, with review by the clinician, can help ensure that patients "feel the success" of the changes they are making. Likewise, activity assignments are frequently done in conjunction with cognitive interventions to manage how patients are interpreting their return to productive and pleasant activities.

Time is also devoted to identifying and increasing pleasant activities that have fallen out of the patient's repertoire. To aid this discussion, the clinician and patient are provided with a list of common pleasant events for consideration (see the Pleasant Event List in the Appendix of Forms and Handouts). The patient is to pick items of most interest, and the clinician helps the patient troubleshoot placement of these pleasant activities in the Weekly Activity Schedule (see Appendix of Forms and Handouts). Patients then monitor their adherence to this program of stepwise increasing activity, and report on associated mood changes.

Box 4.4 Academic Moment: The Success of Behavioral Activation

Behavioral activation offers a very straightforward approach to treating depression: return depressed patients to purposeful and productive activity, and depression will fade. Although clinicians sometimes distrust interventions that seem this straightforward, it is important to realize that it works well. A wealth of evidence supports the efficacy of behavioral activation approaches (see Hopko et al., 2003). For example, a recent large-scale comparative trial examining the relative efficacy of behavioral activation, cognitive therapy, and pharmacotherapy (i.e., paroxetine) found that for patients with more severe depression, behavioral activation and paroxetine offered equivalent outcomes, and both outperformed cognitive therapy (Dimidjian et al., 2006). Other studies found comparable outcomes between cognitive and behavioral activation approaches (Jacobson et al., 1996). Also, behavioral activation treatments, like cognitive interventions, offer strong protection against depressive relapse over 2-year follow-up periods (Gortner et al., 1998) at least equal to that afforded by continuation pharmacotherapy (Dobson et al., 2008). These data encourage serious and regular application of behavioral activation interventions as part of treatment efforts for depressed patients, and underscore the treatment successes that can be brought by doing rather than simply talking.

EXERCISE AS AN ACTIVITY GOAL

As part of activity assignments, the value of exercise cannot be overestimated. Exercise interventions have shown clear efficacy for depression that rivals that for other treatments, including pharmacotherapy (Stathopoulou et al., 2006). There are also initial studies showing benefit for anxiety disorders such as panic disorder (Broocks et al., 1998). Exercise for purposes of mood control, as compared to exercise for general health, also offers up a very different profile and timeline of benefits. Reductions in feelings of stress can immediately follow exercise. These contingent mood benefits also help undo one of the greatest challenges to exercise adherence—not feeling like exercising. When exercising for mood benefits, feeling poorly is the very reason to engage in exercise instead of avoiding it. We believe it to be very important to communicate to patients that the goal of exercise is to feel better *now*. Nonetheless, patients should be assured that when they exercise for mood, not only are they likely to feel better, but they are also more likely to have greater health and a longer life span during which to feel better.

Box 4.5 Academic Moment: The Efficacy of Exercise for Major Depression

In a recent meta-analytic review of 11 trials that compared exercise programs to a non-active comparison condition (e.g., waitlist or placebo treatment, low-level exercise and health education), exercise interventions were associated with a large mean overall between-group effect size (g = 1.39 or d = 1.42), indicating a significant advantage of exercise interventions over control conditions (Stathopoulou et al., 2006). The exercise interventions in these studies varied between two and four times a week, with durations between 20 and 45 minutes. Dropout rates for the exercise interventions were comparable to those observed for psychotherapy and pharmacological interventions; on average, 19.9% of patients did not complete the exercise intervention (Stathopoulou et al., 2006). Comparative treatment trials indicate that there is comparable efficacy between exercise interventions and pharmacotherapy (Blumenthal et al., 1999), and that exercise can be a useful adjunct to ongoing pharmacotherapy (Trivedi et al., 2006).

The target frequency and intensity of exercise prescription for patients with mood or anxiety disorders are consistent with the recent Department of Health and Human Services public health recommendation for aerobic exercise at (1) moderate intensity for at least 150 minutes (2 hours and 30 minutes) each week, or (2) vigorous intensity for at least 75 minutes (1 hour and 15 minutes) each week. Commonly these goals are broken into three or four sessions of exercise each week. Activities such as swimming leisurely, walking at 3 or 4 mph, or playing doubles tennis are considered moderate in intensity; and activities such as jogging or running at greater than 4.5 mph, Rollerblading, and bicycling on a flat surface at greater than 12 mph can be considered vigorous in intensity. In terms of age-adjusted heart rate (HR_{max} = 220 – age), the American College of Sports Medicine (2005) classifies 64% to 76% of HR_{max} as reflecting moderate exercise and 77% to 93% of HR_{max} as reflecting vigorous exercise.

Manualized programs of exercise interventions are available, with both therapist guides (Smits & Otto, 2009) and patient workbooks (Otto & Smits, 2009). A basic guide for patients for structuring exercise interventions for mood and anxiety symptoms is included in the Appendix of Forms and Handouts (Exercise Planning Worksheet) and should be considered as an element of activity and exposure assignments, with careful evaluation of the patient's level of health for these interventions.

5

ADDITIONAL STRATEGIES: PROBLEM-SOLVING
AND RELAXATION TRAINING

In the chapters that follow, core interventions for mood, anxiety, and sleep disorders are described, with guidance in the standard application of specific treatment elements. Missing in these chapters, however, is the rich variation on themes and interventions sometimes necessary to lead a patient into remission. At times, these additional interventions include skill training to help patients better negotiate their lives. For example, although most patients with social anxiety disorder actually do have intact social skills, and instead suffer from an inhibition of their use, some patients do not have an adequate social repertoire. For these patients, modeling and rehearsal of social and assertiveness skills (e.g., introducing oneself at a business meeting or party, or asking someone out on a date) is appropriate, with corrective feedback provided by the clinician. However, provision of this modeling and rehearsal is well outside the brief intervention model at the heart of this book. If such services are needed, these patients can be referred.

Nonetheless, we did not want to move into the diagnosis-based chapters without review of two additional skills: problem-solving and relaxation skills. These skills can be provided in a brief format and are frequently needed in clinical practice.

PROBLEM-SOLVING TRAINING

The need for active problem-solving training may be encountered at any of a number of phases of treatment across different disorders. In depression, for example, a patient's negative and pessimistic view of the present and future may lead him or her to feel trapped with current options, or to feel that no option may work when problems are encountered. These issues can be addressed with cognitive restructuring, but at times the active generation of novel solutions to a problem can act as a more effective means for cognitive change. In other words, an active session of problem-solving training fits the notion of providing change by doing: helping the patient directly discover that more effective alternatives exist and can be applied. In addition, problem-solving training provides a method for addressing the next problem to be encountered. This dual action of cognitive change and skill development in the face of depression may be one reason why treatments emphasizing problem-solving training have demonstrated reliably strong effect sizes for the treatment of major depression that rival those for other cognitive-behavioral interventions or pharmacotherapy (Bell & D'Zurilla, 2009). In addition, problem-solving training is available for the many interpersonal problems that coexist with Axis I disorders, aiding patients in restarting a more active lifestyle after being waylaid by the avoidance that is part of both anxiety and mood disorders.

Active problem-solving training teaches the patient to evaluate and solve problems more efficiently by trying to break habitual ways of responding through engendering consideration of numerous alternatives. In problem-solving training, all potential solutions are considered viable until they are evaluated more closely. The use of problem solving does not guarantee a perfect solution, but does ensure that the patient considers the problem and solutions more thoroughly before making decisions or "giving up."

Components of a traditional problem-solving approach include:

1. Identifying the problem
2. Clearly defining the problem (what about the situation makes it problematic?)
3. Brainstorming a list of all possible solutions, even those that may seem odd or unreasonable
4. Evaluating the solutions (advantages and disadvantages of each)
5. Selecting a solution or combination of solutions
6. Implementing the solution
7. Evaluating the effectiveness of the solution

The goal of this intervention is to teach the overall problem-solving approach to patients, yet encourage the use of individual steps in a less formal manner to address daily problems. The use of individual components of a problem-solving strategy can be modeled in session, and assigned for home application, using the Problem-Solving Worksheet in the appendix (see Fig. 5.1 for a sample completed worksheet). In addition, patients may need help in challenging irrational thinking that impedes effective problem solving.

When helping a patient apply the problem-solving format, perhaps the most important steps are clarifying the nature of the problem (many patients will want to move to the "solve" stage without understanding what it is that is bothering them about the issue) and generating lots of alternatives before moving to evaluate any. In fact, clinicians will need to actively discourage evaluation of solutions until the next step, and reiterate the notion of brainstorming ideas before evaluating them. In the

---

Problem-solving worksheet

What is the problem:

Arguments with my spouse about money

Why does this problem bother me (what are the specific features that bother me)?

I want a better sense of control over our finances.

I feel like I'm the only one who really cares what happens with our money.

Is this a realistic problem (e.g., what do I really think is going to happen, and what part of this problem do I think is just worry)?

Yes, we really argue quite often about money

How can I rewrite the problem clearly, so that it helps me think about a solution? Write in a clear restatement of the problem:

My spouse and I don't plan how to spend money, and then we're surprised by what each of us has spent. This always leads to an argument.

Now that I have the problem clearly in mind, what are potential solutions to this problem? To generate solutions, I want to think about as many possible solutions as possible (without thinking why they are good or bad, and without choosing an option at this point). What advice might a good friend give? If a friend had this problem, what advice would I give?

Potential options:

1. *Just keep doing what we're doing.*

2. *Set up a weekly meeting where my spouse and I can discuss our finances and the household budget.*

3. *Open separate bank accounts.*

4. *Use a notebook to track expenses and review with one another on a weekly basis.*

5. *Assign a small amount of money as "free use" money and create a stricter budget for managing the rest.*

Now rate each potential option. For each option rate the good and bad aspects of the proposed solution. Do not select an option until each is rated.

Figure 5.1 Example of Completed Problem-Solving Worksheet

Good things about each solution	Bad things about each solution
1. <u>No effort required</u>	<u>Nothing is resolved and things may get worse</u>
2. <u>Gives us a chance to talk openly about money</u>	<u>We may end up fighting during meetings</u>
3. <u>Gives each of us a sense of freedom</u>	<u>I would feel like we aren't partners</u>
4. <u>Makes each of us accountable and makes sure we talk to each other about money</u>	<u>May be hard to remember to use the notebook</u>
5. <u>Like option #3, this gives us more freedom</u>	<u>We really should be buying things together, as a couple</u>

Given this evaluation, which solution seems best?

<u>Options 2 and 4 seem like the best solutions. Tracking our finances and meeting weekly seems to be a good way to start changing the situation.</u>

Do you want to apply this solution, or is more time or more information needed to solve this problem?

<u>Yes, I think we can start having meetings and using a notebook to track our finances. I really want to change things and avoid arguments over money.</u>

Figure 5.1 *continued*

case of depression treatment, as the patient becomes aware of a range of potential approaches to the problem, his or her sense of hopelessness may decrease and an affective shift may occur.

It will not be necessary to carry out all steps of the problem-solving strategy with every patient. For example, if a depressed patient has experienced an affective shift and is more open to alternatives, it may not be necessary to assist him in formally carrying out the final steps of problem solving. Rather, at this point you may want to briefly discuss what the patient will do to finish problem solving for this particular situation, and then move on. It is important to include this topic in the agenda for the next session to see how the problem was resolved.

On the other hand, if the patient continues to have difficulty, more time or information may be necessary to solve the problem than is allowed in the session. Help the patient determine what he or she can do to gather more information and revisit the problem during a future session. If the patient does adopt a solution or a combination of solutions, the next step is to formulate a plan for carrying out the solution. The final step of problem solving is to evaluate the effectiveness of the plan and its implementation. This can be an especially rewarding stage, and is done not only to follow through with this initial problem-solving effort but also to encourage future use of this process.

RELAXATION TRAINING

Relaxation training can provide benefit to a broad group of patients with anxiety, anger, sleep, and mood disruptions (see this chapter's Academic Moment). Given these broad-based benefits, relaxation training frequently should be considered as a component intervention; recording an initial relaxation instruction with the patient allows the clinician to move training outside the valuable time of the clinical session. Nonetheless, to enhance adherence, clinicians do need to monitor the application of relaxation training over time.

Our version of relaxation training starts with the classic tense–relax method of teaching patients how to (1) identify the feel of muscular tension and (2) learn how to let that tension go. Although the fuller tense–relax method of moving through select muscle groups provides deep feelings of pleasurable relaxation, the broader goal is to translate the skill of dropping muscle tension into a brief, 10-second procedure that can be used in the moments of everyday life when a shift in emotion and bodily comfort is desirable. This on-the-go relaxation training is used to keep the "relaxation habit" alive, reduce increasing muscular tension across the day, and provide an in-the-moment stress management skill.

Box 5.1 Academic Moment: Relaxation Training

Despite its simplicity, relaxation training remains a powerful intervention for a variety of disorders. For treatment of insomnia (Morin et al., 2006), anger (Del Vecchio & O'Leary, 2004), and worry and generalized anxiety (Gould et al., 2004), including anxiety in late life (Thorp et al., 2009), progressive muscle relaxation training offers clear benefit that rivals other interventions. One exception to this pattern is the differential efficacy for relaxation training versus exposure-based CBT packages for panic disorder, with the latter offering much more beneficial anti-panic effects (Siev & Chambless, 2007). It is not clear how much of the salutary effects of relaxation training are due to the change in arousal versus the generalized benefit of being able to rapidly change one's bodily feelings and affect with a brief relaxation procedure; this ability may substantially increase one's perception of the manageability of emotional experience, regardless of the type of emotion. A prominent example is the role of relaxation training in treating depression. Although inferior to more specific CBT packages for depression, relaxation training does nonetheless offer benefit according to meta-analytic review of studies (Jorm, Morgan & Hetrick, 2008). In part because of its partial efficacy and ease of implementation, Jorm and colleagues (2008) suggested relaxation training may have utility as a first-line treatment in a stepped-care approach to managing depression.

We do want to caution, however, that relaxation should not be used as a strategy to fight against anxiety. Trying *not* to get anxious is one of the best ways we know to actually promote anxious arousal. Instead, we prefer to use relaxation training as a way to become as comfortable as possible while allowing and accepting whatever feelings of anxiety may be present. This is consistent with the overall approach for anxiety-related disorders that we emphasize: anxiety is a signal. The goal is to become comfortable with this signal and to choose adaptive action in the face of it. Accordingly, we tend to think of relaxation training as an overall positive skill that can be applied for general management of stress, anger, worry, insomnia, and over-arousal. A brief method for training relaxation based on broader procedures detailed by Bernstein and Borkovec (1973) is provided in the following section (and is described by Otto & Pollack, 2009).

During individualized training in muscle relaxation, the clinician asks the patient to tense and relax each of a series of individual muscle groups twice. The clinician directs the amount of time tension is held by cueing the patient with the words "tension" and then "relax" approximately 5 to 7 seconds later. The patient is asked to notice the difference in the feeling between the tension and the relaxation phases. Time is taken with this process, with the clinician guiding the patient to notice and enjoy the relaxation phase for approximately 15 to 20 seconds before moving to the next tension phase on the same or a different muscle group. It is important to remind patients that one does not have to induce very much muscle tension to receive the benefits of the procedure; it is often helpful to create just enough tension to "feel it." The important part of the procedure is the process of letting the tension go, and feeling the difference. The tense–relax exercise can be completed for the following muscle groups (unless the patient has a specific pain condition or other physical condition that limits movement or makes these exercises uncomfortable or ill-advised). Each exercise should be performed twice before the patient moves on to the next exercise.

- **Hand Tension:** Tense the hand muscles by making a fist for 5 to 7 seconds.
- **Upper Arm Tension:** Bend the arms by bringing the hands up near the shoulders (tension should be felt in the front of the arms or biceps).
- **Shoulder Tension:** Shrug the shoulders slightly by raising the shoulders toward the ears.
- **Upper Face Tension:** Raise the eyebrows while keeping the eyes closed (lowering the eyebrows can be substituted).
- **Lower Face Tension:** Press the lips together and the teeth together (lightly) while frowning.
- **Chest Tension:** Take a deep chest breath and hold it.

After completing relaxation exercises in session, assign home practice. Be sure to advise the patient of common errors, such as rushing the procedure or not setting aside time to practice. Emphasize to the patient that relaxation training takes just 20 minutes a day. Advise the patient to hold tension for 5 seconds and then relax for 15 seconds. Letting go of the tension is the most important part of the relaxation exercise. Ask the patient to complete a 20-minute practice session each day during the first week of training.

After the patient has practiced the full procedure for a week or two, he or she can begin to practice using a relaxation cue, a 10-second procedure to recall and apply the benefits of muscle relaxation. For the relaxation cue, the patient is to complete just 5 seconds of muscle tension (using a combination of the above procedures, but emphasizing taking a deep breath and tensing the face, shoulders, and hands), followed by letting go of the tension and feeling the difference. The goal is to recall relaxation similar to the full procedure with just this brief cue.

6

CBT FOR PANIC DISORDER

CBT for panic disorder is directed toward breaking the patterns that escalate anxiety into panic by (1) eliminating fears of anxiety sensations and (2) helping patients relearn a sense of safety in avoided situations. To achieve these ends, CBT trains patients to react differently to the somatic, cognitive, and situational cues for panic attacks. In the early stages of treatment, patients learn that panic symptoms are manageable and tolerable. Later in treatment, patients learn to eliminate the regular elicitation of anticipatory anxiety and panic attacks by eliminating the fears underlying panic disorder. The final stages of treatment are aimed at eliminating avoidant patterns and enhancing the pursuit of valued activities. When these steps are completed, patients tend to achieve long-term relief from panic disorder and agoraphobia.

INFORMATIONAL INTERVENTIONS

- Provide an overview of a cognitive-behavioral model of panic disorder.
- Provide information on the role of catastrophic thoughts, and have the patient identify his or her catastrophic interpretations of symptoms.
- Provide instruction in stepwise exposure to avoided situations.
- Monitor exposure progress in follow-up visits.

CORE INTERVENTION ELEMENTS

- Assign monitoring of catastrophic thoughts with attention to the situations that elicit them.

- Review these thoughts, and efforts to correct distortions in thoughts, during sessions.
- Instruct patients in exposure to feared sensations (interoceptive exposure).
- Complete regular in-session interoceptive exposure.
- Assign home practice of interoceptive exposure, with attention to how the patient responds to these sensations.

PROVIDING PATIENTS WITH A COGNITIVE-BEHAVIORAL MODEL OF PANIC DISORDER

In minimal treatment, the clinician is relying on instruction to help the patient mobilize his or her own efforts at eliminating the panic cycle. Figure 6.1 provides an illustration of this cycle, emphasizing the role of the fears and catastrophic misinterpretations of symptoms that are central to the disorder.

It is important to help patients learn the informational interventions linked to this figure that provide the rationale for the treatment interventions to follow, so that they can break their anxiety experience into manageable elements. It is clear to us that patients learn and understand this cycle best if it is self-generated; if you are able to construct the cycle for patients in the context of a clinical discussion about their own experience, patients will rapidly identify the cycle as their own. We believe this

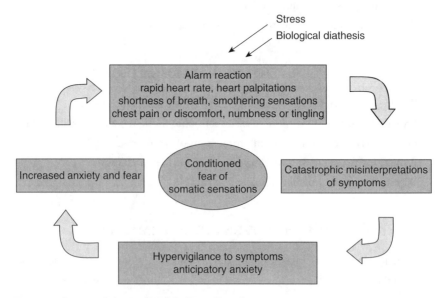

Figure 6.1 Cognitive-Behavioral Model of Panic Disorder

strategy enhances patients' memory of the intervention and helps ensure they can apply it to their own panic disorder.

This discussion between clinician (C) and patient (P) may unfold as follows:

> **C:** When you have a panic attack, what symptoms are most noticeable to you?

Action:

Record the symptoms described by the patient, and then label these symptoms "fight-or-flight" responses. Explain that these symptoms are common fight-or-flight responses, but that at times of actual danger attention is riveted to the source of the danger (e.g., other cars in the case of a near car accident). When these responses fire outside a dangerous situation, something very different happens: the symptoms become a focus of concern in their own right.

> **C:** Now when you have some of these symptoms, what are your thoughts? What do you tell yourself?

Action:

List these cognitions, working to identify the form of these thoughts. These fears may include fears of death and disability ("Am I having a heart attack?" "I might be having a stroke"), fears of loss of control ("What if I have to run out of the room? What if I fall down?"), and fears of humiliation ("They will think I am nuts if I freeze up and can't eat"). A fuller accounting of common catastrophic thoughts among patients with panic disorder is included in Table 6.1. Discuss with the patient that the form or content of these thoughts may have changed over time (e.g., fears of death may have decreased after the disorder was diagnosed or after initial treatment led to some benefits), but a variety of other fears (as per Table 6.1) may remain.

> **C:** Now take a look at some of the thoughts you have listed [*read to patient*]. If anyone had thoughts like these, and believed these, how do you think that person would feel?

Action:

Elicit information about increased symptoms as well as increased vigilance to symptoms. Also discuss the role of memories of past attacks ("I hope it won't be like the time when. . .") and anticipation of increasing symptoms.

> **C:** And if they had increased anxiety, how would that make a person feel?

Action:

Discuss with the patient the self-perpetuating nature of a "fear-of-fear" cycle.

Introducing the panic model with Socratic questioning will help patients develop their own understanding of the panic cycle. It is then complemented by providing the patient with a printed handout of Figure 6.1 (see Appendix of Forms and Handouts) for home review. However, if time is limited, within the context of providing only minimal intervention, clinicians can provide a more didactic instead of a Socratic presentation of this information.

The following dialogue exemplifies some of the information that should be presented as part of a review of the handout. This material would be used to complement the more Socratic presentation or, in the context of a minimal CBT intervention, would form the core of the model presentation. In this example, material is presented as if the clinician is also choosing to prescribe medication for panic disorder.

> **C:** I am going to be giving you some medications that should help you substantially in controlling your anxiety and preventing your panic. In addition, I am going to work with you to show you additional ways to shut down these cycles of panic and to get back to living your life the way you want to. In particular, we are going to work together to reduce your avoidance and increase your involvement in work and social activities that are important to you. To do that, I need to tell you more about some of the most common patterns in panic disorder.
>
> Take a look at this figure. This is a diagram of one of the most typical patterns in panic disorder. It emphasizes that panic disorder involves fears of the physical sensations of anxiety. Here are a few of the sensations that typify a panic attack: [*list some of the sensations reported to you by the patient in the evaluation, such as a rapid heart and breathing rate, dizziness, lightheadedness, and numbness and tingling*]. In panic disorder, the usual response to these sensations is what I call an "uh-oh" response, characterized by a range of fears of the meaning of these sensations. Often these fears are in the form of "what if. . .," including such things as "What if I lose control?" "What if I have a heart attack?" or "What if fall down?" The natural result of these thoughts, if you believe them, is increased attention to the feared sensations and memories of when you had panic attacks before, with such thoughts as "I hope I don't have one of those attacks like I had in December." This increased vigilance and fear of negative outcomes has one primary effect: increased anxiety and panic sensations. Unfortunately, with repetitions this cycle just gets stronger, so it doesn't take much to set off the full pattern—entry into a situation where a panic attack happened before, a rapid heart rate (even if it is from something as simple as climbing stairs), or a worry about a panic symptom.
>
> And this isn't even the worst part: it is often the avoidance of panic situations (the agoraphobic avoidance) that really undoes quality of life.

Table 6.1 Common Anxiogenic Thoughts in Panic Disorder

- Fears of death or disability
  - Am I having a heart attack?
  - I am having a stroke!
  - I am going to suffocate!
- Fears of losing control/insanity
  - I am going to lose control and scream.
  - I am having a nervous breakdown.
  - If I don't escape, I will go crazy.
- Fears of humiliation or embarrassment
  - People will think something is wrong with me.
  - They will think I am a lunatic.
  - I will faint and be embarrassed.

> Now, while we are going to use medication to help control aspects of this cycle, we are also going to implement a plan to get you back to avoided situations, and a plan to help you coach yourself more effectively when you do have some of these sensations, in order to shut down this panic cycle. The first part of this plan is to have you read and work through some handouts on this panic cycle and the thoughts that often go with this cycle. Do you have any questions?

Regardless of the style of informational intervention used, clinicians should make sure their patients understand the role of catastrophic misinterpretations of symptoms in (1) enhancing anticipatory anxiety, (2) eliciting panic attacks, and (3) motivating avoidance. It is important to remember that these catastrophic misinterpretations are one component of the core fears of panic sensations; the model includes helping patients understand that these fearful reactions occur at both a cognitive and automatic level of processing (responding directly with fear to somatic sensations of anxiety). The Common Anxiogenic Thoughts in Panic Disorder handout in the appendix may be helpful in this discussion with patients.

Overall, fears of panic sensations are introduced as a set of cognitions that place individuals at risk for panic onset and help maintain the disorder once established. Additional information on the evidence for the cognitive-behavioral model of panic disorder is provided in the Academic Moment (Box 6.1 below).

Box 6.1 Academic Moment: A Cognitive-Behavioral Model of Panic Disorder

Recurrent panic attacks represent intense anxiety responses that are cued by subjective rather than objective danger, with the assumption that even small emotional, physiological, and behavioral changes become associated with panic attacks, and develop the ability to evoke these responses (Bouton, Mineka & Barlow, 2001). Fears of future panic attacks, heralded in part by exposure to situational or somatic cues of past attacks, help ensure a high level of anticipatory anxiety as well as vigilance to feared sensations. Once symptoms are detected, they are misinterpreted within the context of fears of these sensations, with expectations of catastrophic outcomes, as well as memories of past attacks; the result is a cascade of rising anxiety, apprehension, and panic characterizing a self-perpetuating cycle. Avoidance of situations where panic attacks are feared (e.g., elevators, subway trains, grocery stores) define the agoraphobic subtype, but the patient may also try to avoid internal stimuli that are reminiscent of feared sensations of anxiety and panic (e.g., Salkovskis, Clark & Gelder, 1996). For example, patients with panic disorder may stop exercising because they experience the physiological arousal as too frightening due to its resemblance to a panic attack. One consequence of avoidance is that it prevents individuals from re-establishing a sense of safety in relation to feared sensations or situations.

As evident in Figure 6.1, this account is not inconsistent with a biological diathesis for the disorder, nor with a role for the general life stressors that seem to set the stage for the emergence of recurrent panic attacks, at least as judged by the retrospective report of patients with panic disorder (Manfro et al., 1996). Indeed, there is some evidence to suggest that, at least for women, a heritable component may be linked to the fears of somatic sensations of anxiety that are emphasized by cognitive-behavioral accounts (e.g., Jang, Stein, Taylor & Livesley, 1999). These fears of anxiety sensations, frequently operationalized as high scores on the Anxiety Sensitivity Index, have been shown to be an important predictor of the emergence of panic in response to psychosocial stress, of panic responses to biological provocation, and of risk of relapse in patients with panic disorder (for review see McNally, 2002).

The etiological importance of fear of anxiety sensations is also demonstrated in a study of the prevention of panic disorder. In this study, Gardenswartz and Craske (2001) selected "at-risk" college students based on the presence of fears of anxiety sensations and occasional panic attacks, and examined the efficacy of a 5-hour workshop relative to a waitlist control condition in preventing the onset of panic disorder. Elements of treatment in the workshop included education about the nature and etiology of panic and agoraphobia, cognitive restructuring, exposure to feared somatic sensations (interoceptive exposure), and instructions for *in vivo* exposure to avoided situations (see below for further review of these procedures). Results of the randomized trial indicated that these investigators indeed had selected a high-risk cohort: panic disorder emerged in 13.6% of the individuals in the waitlist condition. Consistent with a model of panic prevention, only 1.8% of those attending the prevention workshop had emergent panic disorder. Studies like this, indicating the ability to both predict and control the emergence of panic disorder in vulnerable individuals, encourage the cognitive-behavioral model of panic disorder and the focus on fears of somatic sensations. Accordingly, CBT protocols offer a combination of informational, exposure, and cognitive restructuring interventions to bring about changes in these core fears and to eliminate some of the responses to symptoms, including avoidance, that help maintain the disorder. Information on fuller treatment protocols can be obtained from a variety of sources (e.g. Barlow, 2004; Barlow & Craske, 2006; Otto & Pollack, 2009).

COGNITIVE RESTRUCTURING

Cognitive restructuring is a natural extension of informational interventions. As patients learn to identify the role of thoughts in the fear-of-fear cycle, the next steps are to help them intervene to (1) change their willingness to believe the negative thoughts that are currently active and (2) develop a more adaptive cognitive repertoire for guiding themselves.

Preparatory skills for cognitive restructuring can be developed by instructing patients to "stop and listen in on" the sorts of things they are saying to themselves. In particular, you want your patients to do this upon increases in anxiety. However, it is not uncommon for patients to have initial difficulty completing cognitive tasks at moments of intense anxiety. For most patients, reactions during a panic attack have become so automatic that it is difficult to evaluate thinking until after the attack has subsided. Hence, cognitive restructuring in panic often involves moving the intervention "backward," starting with post-panic evaluation of thoughts and working over time to notice these thoughts in "real time." This process is aided by preparing patients for the form and content of anxiogenic thoughts. As noted, many of the negative and catastrophic thoughts will be a variant of "What if. . ." (e.g., "What if it gets worse?" "What if it is like last time?" "What if other people notice?"). In other words, the prototypic panic-related thoughts are future-oriented and tend to focus on the perceived consequences of panic sensations.

Although the content of these thoughts may be specific to the patient's particular symptoms and fears (see Table 6.1), negative thoughts associated with anxiety can be categorized broadly into two types of distortions: overestimations of the probability of negative outcomes and overestimations of the degree of catastrophe of these outcomes. Examples follow for the use of Socratic questioning to help patients evaluate the veracity of their negative thoughts. Both of these examples concern fears of fainting associated with panic.

Probability overestimation

C: You mentioned that you are particularly frightened when you get lightheaded or have difficulties focusing during panic attacks. What in particular do you fear will happen at these moments?

P: Well, I just hate the feeling. It is such an odd feeling, and I just know that I'm about to faint.

C: You fear that you are going to faint?

P: Yeah, I'm afraid that at any moment I might just go down, you know.

C: How often during your panic attacks do you have this fear?

P: Just about every time, at least for the last few years.

C: In the last few years, would you say you worry about fainting during panic 70% of the time, 80%, 90%?

P: Oh, I would say at least 90% of the time.

C: OK, and during the last several years how many panic attacks would you say you had?

P: Oh, I don't know. During the last couple of years, I have had a few panic attacks a week... two or three... usually three a week.

C: And do you worry about fainting at other times?

P: Oh yeah, especially when symptoms are just starting... you know, I have just a bit of the jitters and am a little anxious, I often think, "what if get dizzier and faint?"

C: And how often does that happen?

P: A couple of times a week.

C: OK, so help me with my math here [*writing on a pad*]. Over the last two years, 104 weeks, you have had in the neighborhood of 300 panic attacks, and this doesn't count all the panic attacks you had in the years before that. But in the last two years, you have feared, worried, and were fairly certain that you would faint on 90% of those attacks, right? And you also had the worry a couple of hundred other times, when you just had limited symptom episodes?

P: Right.

C: Ok, let's focus on the panic episodes when the feelings are strongest.

P: OK... yeah, that is what really scares me.

C: So writing it all out, you worried that you would faint during 270 of 300 of your panic attacks, right?

P: Right.

C: And in the last two years, during how many panic attacks did you actually faint?

P: Uh. . . none.

C: OK, let me write that rate right here; zero out of 300 panic attacks [*put the two rates next to each other to provide stark contrast—all writing should be done so that patient can observe*].

C: Now given that you are an expert on panic attacks, meaning that you have gone through over 300 of them in the last two years alone, and even though fears of fainting are common during panic attacks, what do you think the true risk of fainting is?

P: I would say that it sure feels like you are going to faint, but that I guess you actually don't.

C: I think that is well said. You have the feeling that you are going to faint, and the fear that you are going to faint, but you don't faint.

P: Yeah. I guess I don't. But maybe it is because I avoid.

C: Well, that is in part why I focused on the actual panic attacks instead of the limited-symptom episodes. You have had really strong panic attacks in the last few years, right?

P: Yeah.

C: And the belief that you would faint during those panic attacks was strong, right?

P: Yes, it was.

C: So given this experience you have with actual strong panic attacks that you did not avoid, what is the evidence that these panic sensations make you faint?

P: I feel like I am going to faint, but so far. . . I guess I don't.

C: Given this expert experience, with over 300 panic attacks, the next time you panic and think you are going to faint, do you want to *believe* these thoughts?

P: No!

C: Here, keep this sheet with these numbers on it, and I want to assure you that after two years of worrying you are going to faint, you are probably going to have that thought next panic attack—but the key is, not letting that thought push you around. Know that you are going to think it ("Uh-oh, I am going to faint") but don't let yourself buy into the thought.

Comment:

Note that in this example, the clinician did not try to have the patient STOP thinking the longstanding thought about fainting. Given all the rehearsal of the thought over the years, there is no reason to go into a head-to-head battle trying to stop this thought—it is strongly habitual. Instead, the clinician focused on helping the patient get some emotional distance from her automatic thought. If the clinician wanted to better prepare the patient to react differently to the thought, he or she might have also said:

C: OK, let's look at these numbers again. On most of your 300 panic attacks over the last couple of years, you have said to yourself, "Uh-oh, I am going to faint." Given all that practice, under the high-stress conditions of a panic attack, I think it is a good bet that you will think exactly that during your next panic attack, don't you?

P: Yeah, the thought just comes to me automatically.

C: OK, let's have you say it aloud here so you are prepared. During your next panic attack you will say—say it with me now—*(loudly)* "Uh-oh, I am going to faint."

P: Uh-oh, I am going to faint.

C: Excellent. Let me have you say that again, with gusto.

P: Uh-oh, I am going to faint. [*Laughs*]

C: In fact, let me have you write down the phrase on this piece of paper, because I am sure you are going to think it. I just don't want this old, tired, and apparently untrue thought to push you around anymore.

[*Patient writes out the thought.*]

C: Alright, take a good look at this thought. You have been thinking it for years, but now you have a chance to start reacting differently to it. The question is whether you are going to let that thought make you miserable. Read if for me a few times.

P: Uh-oh, I am going to faint. Uh-oh, I am going to faint. Uh-oh, I am going to faint...

Comment:

In the preceding example, you see the clinician starting exposure to the negative thought itself, giving the patient a chance to develop other associations to the thought other than the panic that has been rehearsed for years. Sometimes, during a procedure like this, the patient may take additional steps in cognitive restructuring.

P: So it seems kind of silly to keep saying this to myself when I panic.

C: Well, it certainly doesn't help you. My guess is that you will say it fairly automatically for a while out of habit, but after you say it, what might you like to say to yourself that is more accurate?

P: I. . . I could say that it sure feels like I may faint, but that it is just a feeling.

C: I think that is a much truer description of what is going on.

Overestimations of the degree of catastrophe

The preceding example was specific to the overestimation of the probability of negative outcomes. Patients also overestimate the degree of catastrophe of outcomes. Here
is another sample dialogue between clinician and patient concerning this other form
of anxiogenic thinking.

> **C:** So you really fear the possibility of fainting?
>
> **P:** Oh, yeah, I could not bear it if I fainted in public.
>
> **C:** What do you mean you could not bear it?
>
> **P:** Oh, it would be simply horrible.

Comment:

Notice that the patient did not provide any specifics on why this experience
is feared, but instead stayed with global descriptions of intolerable states. This
cognitive style is both common in panic disorder and an excellent way to keep
fears alive—global negative consequences that are stated in a way that forestalls
any coping attempts.

> **C:** Tell me what you mean by horrible. What would actually happen?
>
> **P:** Well, I would fall down.
>
> **C:** Yes. . .
>
> **P:** And that would be hugely embarrassing.
>
> **C:** So one negative aspect of fainting in public is that you would fall down and it
> would be embarrassing for you. What do you picture happening?
>
> **P:** I would fall down and, oh, I don't know, people would point and laugh or
> think I was crazy or incompetent or something.
>
> **C:** Do you suppose that is what most people think if they would see someone
> suddenly faint?
>
> **P:** Well, they would think something is wrong.
>
> **C:** I would think so, but what about the crazy or incompetent part?
>
> **P:** Well, they would think something is wrong, and I guess want to help.
>
> **C:** So they would come over to help, and that would be the embarrassing part?
>
> **P:** Well, I would be the center of attention.
>
> **C:** Yes, if you fainted, you would be the center of attention for awhile. Have you
> ever done something embarrassing and been the center of attention?
>
> **P:** Well, yes, you know I've told you I am something of a klutz, but this would be
> different, because this would be a sign of a problem.
>
> **C:** Yes, people would be concerned and might wonder what is wrong. Would
> everyone react that way?
>
> **P:** No, some wouldn't care. Others would wonder what happened.

C: And as a possible consequence of fainting, could you cope with that—being the center of attention, and having some people wonder what happened later?

P: I would not like it.

C: No, you would not like it. But does it sound like an intolerable event that justifies all the panic you experience worrying about the possibility?

P: Hell, sitting here now, I would rather faint than panic.

C: Hmmm. . . Given these thoughts, the next time you have the thought, "Uh-oh, I am going to faint," how do you want to react to it?

As is clear from these dialogues, the clinician must be patient enough to continue helping patients get a clearer conceptualization of their fears and to provide their own answers regarding the degree of catastrophe of the actual event. To help patients decide if they can actually cope with the event, should it occur, the clinician asks questions such as:

- And could you cope with that if it actually happened?
- Have you ever had something like that happen before?
- If you saw that happen to someone else, what would you think (do)?

Clinicians do need to make sure that they do not ask these questions until the patient gets very specific about what she fears happening. In other words, it makes far less sense to ask the question about global negative descriptors (e.g., "And could you cope with something simply horrible?") than a specific outcome (e.g., "And could you cope with being the center of attention?").

In completing cognitive restructuring interventions, clinicians will need to decide whether to focus more on the probability of the negative outcome or its degree of catastrophe, or both. For feared events like heart attacks or strokes, it is natural to focus on the probability of the event. For other events (e.g., being embarrassed), focusing on the degree of catastrophe is more useful. Also, not infrequently patients may need to evaluate the cost of their continued fear versus the possibility of a truly bad outcome (e.g., fearing death from a heart attack on a daily basis and panicking regularly vs. "taking a chance" on this remote outcome and more fully engaging in the joy of life). In all cases, clinicians need to evaluate the true health of their patients in helping them develop accurate thoughts about the meaning of physical sensations.

In all cognitive restructuring efforts, we think it is useful to help patients develop an ability to *marvel* at the degree of negativity of their thoughts. This is done to gain emotional perspective on these thoughts and their function (e.g., "Wow, listen to what I am saying to myself! These are really negative scary thoughts. Do I really want to keep coaching myself that way?" or "Wow, it is really hard on me to keep thinking this way! These thoughts could keep *anyone* scared and vigilant—that is, if they believe them").

INTEROCEPTIVE (INTERNAL CUE) EXPOSURE

Exposure interventions, either interoceptive or *in vivo*, provide patients with crucial learning experiences for evaluating the accuracy of feared beliefs and expectations. As such, during exposure, patients need to pay attention to what *actually* happens, not just what they fear *might* happen. To do so, patients need to be alert and paying attention to actual outcomes, particularly outcomes other than their own symptom experience. This is in part why interoceptive exposure is so crucial in the treatment of panic disorder. As long as anxiety symptoms are believed to be intolerable outcomes in themselves, patients are at the mercy of their own limbic systems and environmental cues. By providing step-by-step experiences in reacting differently to sensations of anxiety, you are providing essential training in emotional acceptance and tolerance.

In the treatment of panic disorder, the goal is to use interoceptive exposure to help patients become comfortable *with* symptoms, instead of being comfortable only in the absence of symptoms. To achieve this outcome, patients will need directed experiences with noticing exactly what feared symptoms feel like in and of themselves (independent of the feared *meaning* of these symptoms). In other words, dizziness as a sign of an impending "horrible and intolerable" event is fairly intolerable, but dizziness as a *sensation* is readily tolerable. Interoceptive exposure is designed to help patients feel the difference between these two ways of experiencing dizziness. As a procedure, interoceptive exposure involves four steps:

1. Preparing patients for the sensations they are about to feel, with attention to normalizing these sensations
2. Inducing the sensations
3. Helping patients to not engage in "protective" (e.g., avoidant) actions during the exposure, and to pay attention to the actual sensations
4. Discussing what was learned from the exposure

Table 6.2 provides a list of common exposure exercises. For these exercises, the presumption is that the clinician has considered the state of fitness of the patients. For example, head rolling is done only after loosening up the neck muscles with gentle stretching, and is not performed in individuals with neck injuries. Likewise, stair running is done with consideration of the appropriate fitness (for pace), coordination, and physical fragility of a patient.

Table 6.2 Common Interoceptive Exposure Procedures

Exposure Procedure	Sensations Commonly Induced
Head Rolling Turning the head around in a circle (from midline, moving down and around and back to midline) with the eyes closed for 20 seconds	Dizziness and disorientation
Hyperventilation Breathing once per second for a minute, taking care to blow off the air	Dizziness, numbness and tingling, hot flushes, visual distortions
Stair Running Climbing rapidly up a few flights of stairs	Breathlessness, pounding heart, heavy legs, trembling
Chair Spinning Spinning around several times in a swivel chair with eyes closed	Strong dizziness and disorientation
Mirror (or Hand) Staring Staring intently in a mirror (or into the palm) for one minute (not allowing the eyes to move)	Derealization
Full-Body Tension Tension from clenching the toes, pressing the heels down, pulling in the stomach, clenching the hands, arms, and (lightly) jaw and brow. Hold this tension for one minute.	Trembling, numbness and tingling, heavy muscles

In interoceptive exposure, we often start with a manageable, common, and easy-to-induce sensation, as illustrated in the following dialogue between clinician (C) and patient (P).

C: In a few moments, I am going to ask you to induce some feelings of dizziness. We will do this by having you move your head around in a circle like this [*clinician models for the patient*] while keeping your eyes closed. When a person does this for more than a few seconds, feelings of dizziness start. For example. . . [*pause*]. . . now I am starting to feel some light dizziness. . . [*pause*]. . . yes, I feel a little odd and off-center. . . [*pause*]. . . and when I stop and open my eyes, the world appears to move a bit in front of me, and then starts looking normal again. And you will notice that I kept breathing while I did this; there is no reason to hold your breath while head rolling. How does this look as something to do?

P: I don't want to do it. I hate being dizzy.

C: Yes, I thought you would say this. You had mentioned that dizziness is part of what you fear about panic, and that is exactly why I want you to have some practice seeing if you can experience dizziness differently.

P: I just don't want it to get out of control.

C: Well, during the procedure I want to give you a chance to find out what dizziness itself feels like. And I would like to give you a chance to tell me what is so bad about it. Before we start, I would like to have you loosen up your neck (the goal of head rolling is dizziness, not a stiff neck), so please go ahead and stretch gently forward, then back, then side to side. And when you complete head rolling, I would like you to start with your head straight up, and then roll your head down and around back to where you started; there is no need to stretch your head backward. Also, many people will start to hold their breath during this procedure. There is no need to do this either. Breathe while you head-roll. OK, go ahead and start.

[*The patient is head rolling.*]

C: Notice what it feels like to get dizzy. Let it happen.

[*The patient stops suddenly and grabs the arms of the chair.*]

P: Oooh. I hate that!

C: What did you feel?

P: I'm not sure; I just needed it to stop.

C: Ah, it seems we activated your fear of dizziness, but that you did not get a chance to see why it is so bad.

P: Well, I wanted to stop it before it got worse.

C: So you were afraid of what you might feel.

P: Yes.

C: But what was so bad about what you *did* feel?

P: Well, it felt weird.

C: Weird. . . what was so bad about weird?

P: I'm not sure. I just didn't want things to get out of control.

C: OK, so there are two parts here. Feeling weird, and the things you are saying to yourself about feeling weird, including the fear of what feeling weird might lead to.

P: Yeah.

C: I would like you to head-roll again, but this time, let yourself feel weird and ask yourself what is so bad about feeling weird. Notice what it feels like here and now to feel weird, or dizzy, or odd, or lightheaded, OK?

P: I'll try.

[Initiate head rolling for 20 seconds]

C: What did you notice?

P: I felt weird, and dizzy.

C: Tell me about weird and dizzy. What was so bad about it?

P: Well, I guess it wasn't so bad. It was odd, but I didn't want to panic or anything.

C: So again your thoughts tend to get ahead of your sensations, but you did get a chance to notice that feeling weird wasn't so intolerable.

P: Right.

C: Did you have times in the past when you used to feel weird or dizzy but didn't fear it? For example, as a kid, did you ever try to get dizzy on purpose, perhaps by spinning around in a circle?

P: *[Smiles]* I did do that as a kid.

C: How would you say those feelings as a kid differed from what you are feeling today?

P: *[Pauses]* That is strange. As a kid, I loved them, but now I hate the same sensations.

C: It is fairly common in panic to learn to hate these sensations, but I do want you to get a chance to undo this effect. I would like you to complete head rolling. Again, pay attention to the symptoms, but this time I would also like you to remember what it was like when you were a kid and you used to do this for fun.

[Patient head-rolls.]

C: Well, what did you feel?

P: You know, I felt dizzy and odd, but it wasn't so bad. I thought, so what?

C: Great, this is a crucial part of what you are going to learn in treatment. If you give yourself a chance to see what some of these sensations are actually like, you will find that your fear of them goes away.

Comment:

This dialogue exemplifies the difficulty many patients have in letting themselves experience the sensation, and the efforts a clinician has to make to refocus them on the sensation rather than their experience with the sensations. The clinician also used the patient's own history with the symptom to help her start to process the sensations differently (using a childhood memory). In this way, the clinician gave the patient her first experience with gaining a sense of safety *with* the feared sensations. This process is exemplified in Figure 6.2. Interoceptive exposure gives patients an opportunity to repeatedly confront the feared sensation and learn a sense of safety. By doing so, the patient is starting to undo the self-perpetuating panic cycle, and to develop a new way of reacting to symptoms.

The goal of repeated exposures is to first help patients get comfortable with the feared sensations in the clinician's office, and then to practice these exposures at home. For example, following the preceding dialogue, the clinician may say:

> **C:** OK, your goal until I see you next time is to practice the sensations daily, trying to get bored with dizziness so that your reaction to these symptoms is more automatically, "Big deal, I am dizzy."

The reason we start with a relatively straightforward induction is so that the patient can experience the difference in reactions to symptoms, and have a "map" for how to complete the homework at home.

As the patient becomes more comfortable with one sensation, the clinician "ups the ante" and rehearses a more difficult sensation with the patient, again sending the patient home to complete exposures on a daily basis until the next session. Also, as

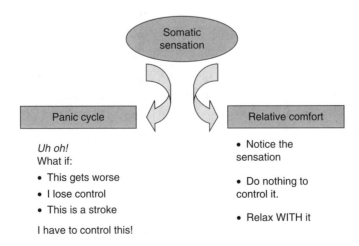

Figure 6.2 Retraining Responses to Anxiety and Panic Symptoms

patients become more comfortable with sensations, many will engage family members in the exposure. They do this to (1) show other family members pieces of what they have been feeling and (2) make the exposures a more social experience.

Occasionally, patients may fail to make a link between interoceptive exposures and more spontaneous sensations. An intervention around this difficulty may unfold as follows.

P: Of course I feel OK with these sensations; I know I have brought them on. When I panic, the sensations just come out of the blue. I don't know why the hell they are there.

C: But the sensations are similar?

P: Yeah, they are similar, but it is totally different when they come out of the blue. I can't stand that.

C: So you are telling me that although the sensations are similar, you are really comfortable with the sensations that you induce, but frightened of the ones that come out of the blue?

P: Yeah, I really fear them when I don't know why they are there.

C: So, the difference between feeling comfortable and feeling panic is that you know how the sensations were induced?

P: Exactly.

C: Well, you are on to something extremely valuable here. What is it you do with the sensations you induce that leads you to be so comfortable?

P: I guess I just tell myself that it is just dizziness.

C: And with the other sensations?

P: I guess I get bent all out of shape asking myself why and trying to make them go away.

C: OK. My bet is that with a little more experience, you will start seeing cues for the "out-of-the-blue" sensations you feel—you know, things you have thought or have just done which may have increased your arousal. But in the meantime, I would like you to start applying this extraordinary ability you have in being comfortable with symptoms that you purposefully brought on, to the symptoms you experience without exactly knowing their cause.

P: I guess I could try that.

As treatment progresses, the clinician continues to target symptoms that are still bothersome to the patient by providing interoceptive exposure practice with the appropriate exercises. Patients should also get practice with the sensations away from their "safe zones" (e.g., doing practice only at home when their spouse is present). To help patients learn a true sense of safety, they should eventually practice sensations when home, when at the store, when others are present, when alone, when tired, when sad, when happy, etc. Indeed, out-of-home exposures are often the most valuable for helping patient truly learn not to fear symptoms. The Exposure Planning Checklist in the appendix is designed to help guide such exposure planning.

TIME LIMITATIONS AND INTEROCEPTIVE EXPOSURE

As should be clear from the preceding pages, providing patients with valuable interoceptive exposure training does take time. We think it is a crucial procedure for ending aspects of the panic cycle, but when clinical time is limited, we would like clinicians to consider at least minimal training in reacting differently to symptoms. Patients can be provided with minimal practice with interoceptive exposure in session, with requests for further practice as per the *in vivo* exposure session to follow. Alternatively, clinicians can use the principles of interoceptive exposure in session as a brief intervention in response to in-session episodes of anxiety.

> **C:** You have said that you are feeling fairly anxious now, is that right?
>
> **P:** Yes, I've been anxious all afternoon, but I haven't panicked yet.
>
> **C:** How are you experiencing your anxiety now; if you had to locate it in your body, where would it be?
>
> **P:** Well, it's in my chest and stomach. It feels fluttery. And I feel jumpy.
>
> **C:** What do you mean by jumpy?
>
> **P:** Well, it's like my arms feel too light or too zingy or something. It is a light sensation, but I hate it because it says I am not in control, and that I just can't calm down.
>
> **C:** OK, I would like you to take a moment and consider what you are doing to manage these sensations now. Are you doing anything to try to control these sensations?
>
> **P:** I do notice that I monitor them. I hoped they would stop when I got in your office, and they didn't, and I keep checking them and thinking, "How long is this going to last?"
>
> **C:** OK, see also if you are doing something right now to manage these sensations.
>
> **P:** [*Pauses*] It. . . uh. . . feels like I am trying to hold on, you know. . . like I have to keep pressing down on the feeling in my chest to keep it from taking over.
>
> **C:** Alright, let's give you a brief break from that. For the next two minutes, I would like you to let your body be as anxious as it wants to be, and instead of trying to control this anxiety—trying to press down on it—I would like you to get as comfortable as you can WITH the anxiety. OK?

P: Uh, OK.

C: Let the anxiety be there, let your chest feel full, your arms feel zingy, and your job is to lean back in your chair, take a deep breath, and see if you can get lazy with these sensations of anxiety. See if you can be comfortable with these sensations.

[*Silence as the patient focuses on internal sensations*]

C: How does this feel?

P: It is odd. It is hard to stop pressing back on these sensations.

C: Keep getting lazy. You must have had odd sensations before. Let these anxiety sensations be experienced like any other sensations. Compare them to knee pain or headache pain so that you can think of your anxiety as a sensation, as a signal that today you don't need to do anything about, and that it is OK to go ahead and relax with these sensations.

[*Silence*]

C: I just saw you drop your shoulders; it actually looks like, as part of trying to control your anxiety, you tense your body. This may actually create some of the very sensations you are trying to avoid. Go ahead and keep letting yourself get comfortable with the sensations of anxiety you have.

P: It is odd. I feel better, even though I still have that feeling in my chest.

[*Silence*]

P: My arms feel better. Actually, I feel better generally.

C: OK, think of this as your first rehearsal of a new approach to your anxiety.

Box 6.2 Academic Moment: Relaxing with Anxiety

Relaxing *with* the sensations of anxiety is very different than relaxing *to try to control* anxiety. The former is designed to reduce anxious reactions to anxiety and promote *acceptance* of these sensations. Rather than involving any formal procedure, in this context "relax" means do nothing to control the sensations, including such things as tensing up. Compared to promoting acceptance, relaxing to try to control anxiety and prevent panic may actually maintain fears of anxiety sensations ("I have got to calm down"). In fact, there is evidence that elimination of relaxation training or breathing retraining has no negative effects on the efficacy of CBT (e.g., Schmidt et al., 2000).

It is important to note the degree to which interoceptive exposure aids cognitive change. With tolerable experiences with symptoms, patients have greater evidence to dispute their catastrophic expectations. Accordingly, clinicians should take a moment to help this process along with questions like the following:

> **C:** What do you make of this exposure? Do you want to keep telling yourself what you usually tell yourself about symptoms like dizziness?

Also, clinicians should not hesitate to underscore the difference in intensity, frequency, or duration of symptoms depending on the reactions to the symptoms:

> **C:** A few weeks ago, these sensations used to really frighten you. You are really making progress with changing the degree to which these symptoms can push you around.

Or:

> **C:** As you have been becoming comfortable with these symptoms, I do want you to notice that your number of weekly panic attacks has been decreasing, and during the few attacks you did have, you said they were much more tolerable. I want you to keep this process going by continuing to practice getting comfortable with symptoms in multiple situations.

USE OF PRN MEDICATIONS WITH EXPOSURE

As should be clear from efforts to help patients practice interoceptive exposure in multiple situations, the degree of safety patients learn with sensations is dependent on the context. If they practice interoceptive exposure only at home, comfort is likely to develop with the sensations primarily at home. Likewise, if patients practice interoceptive exposure only with the clinician, a sense of safety with sensations will likely be conditional to the presence of the clinician. Of course, similar effects can be expected with medication use. If interoceptive exposure is practiced only after taking a pill, then safety with these sensations is likely to be specific to pill-taking (or chronic medication use).

To help your patients learn broader safety, divorce exposure practices from pill use by eliminating PRN use over time (or by never initiating it). Also, if you have applied CBT while the patient is on medication, know that a booster course of CBT during and after medication taper (if it occurs) will help your patient extend and maintain treatment gains.

Box 6.3 Academic Moment: Medications and CBT for Panic

The loss of CBT efficacy upon medication discontinuation, relative to sustained treatment gains among patients who were treated by CBT alone, has been documented in large-scale treatment trials (Barlow et al., 2000; Marks et al., 1993). This loss of efficacy has been interpreted as a context effect, where some of the gains of CBT are specific to the medication context where they were learned (for review see Otto, Smits & Reese, 2005). Other studies have indicated that the application of CBT across medication taper and discontinuation helps patients maintain treatment gains. Accordingly, if patients learn CBT in the context of pharmacotherapy, clinicians should consider fading medication while the patient remains in CBT, or consider referral to CBT if a decision to discontinue medication is made in the future. Specialized protocols for benzodiazepine discontinuation in panic disorder are also available if difficulties tapering this medication are encountered (Otto & Pollack, 2009).

SITUATIONAL (*IN VIVO*) EXPOSURE

In vivo exposure provides patients with opportunities to re-enter and relearn a sense of safety in avoided situations. Cognitive interventions are useful for helping the patient prepare for exposure. Accurate cognitive coaching should be used to help patients reduce anticipatory anxiety before their exposures, but also as a way to guide their attention to how they are actually doing during the exposures. During exposure, the key is to reduce exclusive attention to symptoms by also noticing what is actually going on in the situation, and focusing on completing personal goals linked to the situation (e.g., the goal is not simply to be in the mall for 30 minutes, but to go to the mall for 30 minutes and look at the items in the new store that the patient has been wanting to visit).

In designing situational exposure interventions for your patient, start where he or she is—that is, design an initial exposure that is only moderately harder than current functioning. The goal of initial exposure is to help the patient develop accurate expectations about what the process of successful exposure feels like, and to learn to meet goals in feared situations despite having symptoms. Realize that exposures can be modulated by adjusting the degree of threat of relatively small elements of the experience. For a given patient, the time of day, length of a drive, degree of traffic, the presence of a trusted other, the presence of a cell phone, or length of time until the next clinical session can all be important variables in determining the difficulty of an exposure. Hence, the clinician needs to take some time to be specific: at what time of day, with whom, in what area, and with what goal in mind will an exposure be completed?

Prior to an exposure, the patient should have accurate expectations about what the exposure will be like. We expect patients are likely to have anticipatory anxiety symptoms, and for that reason, we prefer to conduct at least a minimal interoceptive exposure practice prior to initiation of situation exposure. However, when this cannot be arranged, please take the time to have a brief discussion of likely symptoms with your patient.

> **C:** As we discussed, we are going to use exposure to help you maximize your gains in response to your pharmacotherapy. In exposure therapy, I am going to give you practice with re-entering and *winning back* for yourself situations that you have been avoiding. You have told me that you want to get back to driving on the interstate instead of the small local roads.
>
> **P:** Yes, I can save lots of time getting to work, or getting over to my in-laws. And it just feels, you know, like I should be able to do it.
>
> **C:** OK, so you have some clear goals for what you personally are going to get as you invest some time into these exposure procedures.
>
> **P:** Yes.
>
> **C:** What is your sense of what it will be like to start driving again?
>
> **P:** I am very scared by the whole thing. It has been years since I have been on the highway, and all the cars just seem to whiz by so fast.
>
> **C:** OK, so there are many parts to being on the highway. The sense of speed as you drive faster, the sense of other cars around you. . . things like that?
>
> **P:** Yeah, I think all of those things will make me nervous.
>
> **C:** I do think you will be nervous the first few times you try driving on the highway; that would be natural—to be nervous until you get back in the swing of things. To make things easier though, we might do this in several steps.
>
> **P:** OK.
>
> **C:** When you think about getting back on the highway, we can make the exposure easier or harder by having you go at a busy time or a quiet time, of having you drive in the right lane, or cross over to the center lane, or to do it with a friend in the car or with someone waiting for you at home. To start with an exposure that is just moderately hard, what elements do you want in your exposure practice?

P: Well, I am not ready for busy traffic, or night driving, so I guess I would like to go midday on the weekend.

C: OK, do you have a sense of how many exits you want to take so you have a chance to see what it is like? That is, I want you to have several minutes of driving so that you can get a sense of what it is like.

P: Oh, I was thinking more like one exit.

C: Well, if you did just one quick exit, how do you think it will feel?

P: [*Laughs*] I think I would just get on the highway and hold my breath till it's over.

C: Hmmm. . . probably not the experience we are looking for. We do want you to be on the highway long enough to breathe, look around, get over the initial peak of anxiety just as you enter the highway (you know, the "oh-my-gosh, I-am-doing-it, I-am-doing-it, I-am-doing it; am-I-anxious?, am-I-anxious? am-I-anxious?" stage). [*Patient laughs.*] I want you to have a chance to say, "So this is what it's like to be on the highway, looking around, and driving at a reasonable speed experience," even if you are anxious while you are doing it.

P: OK, that makes sense. . . I guess I could go up to Route 7 and then back, that would give me a few minutes of trying it.

C: Excellent. And how about other people? Will you do this by yourself?

P: Yes, I think I would like to try it myself. I get more uptight when my family is in the car.

C: OK, and let's make sure you don't do anything that makes driving harder. When you are in the car with your family or friends over the next few days, I want you to notice where you are looking on the highway. Sometimes when people are anxious they look just over the hood of the car. Check out where you are looking when you are the passenger, and if you are comfortable, chat about it with the driver.

Comment:

In an ideal format, the clinician would precede this intervention with information, rudimentary cognitive restructuring, and practice with interoceptive exposure. The value of interoceptive exposure is that it makes some of the symptoms of anticipatory anxiety less worrisome (I am feeling a little dizzy, but I have gotten good at doing what I need to do while being dizzy). This sort of preparation can also reduce driving errors due to anxiety—that is, with interoceptive exposure you know your patient has experience with behaving normally while dizzy.

With every exposure assignment, it is crucial to ask about progress during the next session. Do not forget to ask! Remember that you have asked the patient to do something he or she fears, and your credibility and your patient's willingness to try the next exposure is linked to your ability to follow up and show interest in your patient's progress and experiences during exposure. We recommend recording the exact exposure assignment in your progress notes to cue your asking about these experiences during the next session. Also, devote a few moments to asking your patient what was learned from the experience. Did the patient remain in the situation and focus on goal attainment? Did relative comfort develop in the situation across the exposure practice?

CHARACTERISTICS OF EXPOSURE SESSIONS

With each exposure, you would like your patient to remain in the situation long enough for anticipatory anxiety to diminish. A good rule of thumb is to have the patient remain in the situation at least twice as long as it takes to become comfortable in that situation. For example, after the patient has completed an initial exposure to learn the basics of the procedure, the patient should plan to stay in situational exposure situations (especially those other than driving [e.g., malls, public places]) for a total of 30 to 60 minutes. It often takes 15 to 20 minutes for initial anticipatory anxiety to dissipate, and hence for ideal exposure the patient should remain in the situation for an additional 30 to 40 minutes. During that time, the patient should focus on goal-directed activity ("let me really let myself watch this movie," "I am going to shop for something for my son," "I am going to notice other conversations in this hair salon, not just think about whether I am trembling"). In addition, don't let exposure be a rare experience. Patients learn well from repetition, and if exposure represents only a rare and well-anticipated experience, the development of comfort in that situation will be delayed.

As your patient's confidence grows in exposure situations, new exposures should be devised, and likewise the degree of safety cues can be reduced. Patients who are traveling with safety cues like cell phones or water bottles can be encouraged to travel without these items (unless true safety considerations dictate otherwise). Also, as detailed in the section on interoceptive exposure, clinicians will have to consider the role of medication in creating a unique context for exposure. Fading PRN use as well as the presence of significant others during exposure will help patients develop a broader sense of safety. The Exposure Planning Checklist in the appendix (see also Chapter 4) is provided for use in planning of exposure assignments.

SIGNS OF ADAPTIVE CHANGE

If treatment is progressing well, clinicians should be vigilant to three types of adaptive change and should adjust interventions to promote these sorts of changes.

The first reflects a crucial change resulting from both interoceptive exposure and cognitive interventions. It is the patient's ability to separate the experience of emotions and sensations from his or her emotional or behavioral response to those experiences. The most direct example of this ability is the patient's comfort with interoceptive exposure sensations produced in the office. Patients may begin to smile in response to exposure inductions as they realize their enhanced comfort (lack of fear) with the induced sensations. Patients may also lean forward and more vigorously discuss their changed experience ("you know, I am dizzy but it isn't so bad—I don't like it, but I don't need to fear it"). More importantly, patients who are progressing well in treatment may begin to report changes in comfort with sensations outside of therapy. This is sometimes evidenced by an enhanced ability to both think through panic situations and to discriminate and tolerate emotional experiences as they occur. This may be expressed as an enhanced ability to identify everyday cues for panic that were once mysterious. In relation to somatic cues, a patient may say:

> I was at the office Monday, and I was looking for an old file that was in my bottom file drawer. I must have stood there looking for about five minutes, bending over at the waist to look into the bottom drawer. Then, when I straightened up, I felt panic sensations. I started to think, "oh no, here it comes," when I realized that I was just feeling lightheaded from having my head down near my knees. It was just like the exposure we did in session, but I think I never realized that sometimes I create similar sensations by accident.

In relation to emotional cues for panic, a patient may say:

> I had a really interesting experience several days ago. My husband and I got into an argument and instead of backing off when he got mad, I continued to try to get him to see my point. When we finally stopped arguing, I went in the bedroom, and I was crying and I started to panic. And then suddenly I thought, I am pissed, not scared. I realized I was trembling, but it was because I was mad. I think I used to panic every time I got upset, even if I was upset for a good reason. Now, I was upset, crying, and thought, "I am upset for a reason; there is no reason to panic about it." I then felt better. I was upset, but I was comfortable being upset.

Likewise, patients may report more general comfort with more subtle emotional provocations from others. For example, a patient may report more comfort interacting with his teenage son because the emotions produced by the conflicts with his son are more emotionally tolerable. With greater tolerability, there is less reason to avoid or terminate (e.g., with authoritarian anger) these interactions.

The second sign of change is more dispassionate responses to anxiety-related thoughts. This change also marks the success of exposure and cognitive interventions. Patients may start to smile, nod, or shake their heads in response to realizing the disparity between their thoughts or expectations and actual outcomes. Clinicians can play a valuable role in underscoring these changes by asking patients to recall past predictions about anxiety and its consequences, and underscoring changes in these attitudes as they occur. These cognitive changes are not more important than accompanying behavioral changes (e.g., reductions in agoraphobia), but they do signify an important and broader attitudinal change in beliefs about panic that may help patients generalize their anxiety-reduction efforts.

Finally, a later-stage signifier of change is the patient's report of the re-emergence of fun on outings. With reductions in agoraphobic avoidance (if present) and reductions in fear of symptoms, patients will often spontaneously report a joyful return to missed activities. If this does not occur, patients may need planning for a more active re-entry into once-avoided situations, including rehearsal of what used to be pleasurable about these situations. Re-attending to joy is a skill that may be lost for patients due to the longstanding vigilance to feared outcomes that is part of chronic panic disorder. As noted in Chapter 2, adding a well-being component to treatment can help patients re-develop a focus on what is working well in life and in planning for additional periods of pleasure.

7

CBT FOR DEPRESSION

For the goal of treating depression, you have at hand two fundamental interventions: (1) increasing valued activity and (2) changing thoughts that maintain depression. Regarding activity, research has documented that restoration of valued activities (pleasurable events and goal attainment) is a potent antidepressant. In addition, exercise alone can have some powerful antidepressant effects, rivaling outcomes for both antidepressants and CBT. Likewise, a large body of research documents the efficacy of cognitive restructuring interventions in the treatment of depression. As such, the overall goal of CBT for major depression is to restore healthy thinking and behavior patterns to break the cycle of negative expectations and negative evaluations, and the low rates of rewarding activities that characterize depression. To achieve these ends, CBT provides patients with training in identifying and changing negative thoughts and in planning and accurately evaluating pleasant events and rewarding and productive activities.

INFORMATIONAL INTERVENTIONS

- Provide an overview of the role of negative thinking styles in maintaining depression.
- Provide training in challenging and restructuring negative thoughts.
- Provide instruction in stepwise scheduling of rewarding activities.
- Monitor progress in follow-up visits.

CORE INTERVENTION ELEMENTS

- Assign monitoring of negative thoughts with attention to the events that elicit them.
- Review these thoughts and efforts to challenge them during sessions.
- Instruct patients in appropriately challenging or restructuring negative thoughts (cognitive restructuring).
- Complete regular in-session review of rewarding activities.
- Assign home practice of engaging in rewarding activities, with attention to how participating in such activities relates to depressive symptoms.

PROVIDING PATIENTS WITH A COGNITIVE-BEHAVIORAL MODEL OF DEPRESSION

With minimal treatment, the clinician is relying on instruction to help the patient mobilize his or her own efforts at eliminating self-perpetuating patterns within depression. By instructing patients in the common cognitive styles that characterize depression, the clinician is trying to help the patient gain perspective on these thoughts, and to mobilize efforts at more accurate and effective thinking. Likewise, by focusing on a stepwise return to productive and rewarding activity, the clinician is providing instruction in self-care and actions that are incompatible with maintained depression.

The goal of cognitive restructuring is for the patient to develop a different response to negative cognitions, while working over time to change the nature of these thoughts. This process involves the development of a new awareness of the destructive role of negative thoughts in mood and activity management. Patients are to learn to listen in and alter their self-talk. Like other cognitive and affective interventions, this process is aided by the ability to "marvel" at these thoughts while structuring a change in their content ("Oh my gosh! Look how negative that thought is; imagine the mood hit I would take if I bought into this thought. What is a more useful thought I can use to guide myself?").

Classic cognitive restructuring for depression (see Beck, 1995) includes instruction in the role of thoughts, monitoring of automatic thoughts, instruction in identifying cognitive errors, and substituting alternative thoughts. For example, the clinician may say:

> As part of treating your depression, I am going to have you pay extra attention to your thoughts and how you react to your thoughts. In depression, thoughts tend to become especially negative and self-critical, with negative expectations about the present and future. Also, beliefs that you may not have while you are not depressed become more influential when you are depressed.

Beliefs about feeling flawed, feeling unlovable, and needing to be perfect for acceptance can all become more dominant when you are depressed. These thoughts have the effect of hurting your mood, decreasing your motivation, and making effort seem worthless. As part of treatment, we will be seeing what sort of thoughts you are having, especially when your mood is bad, and we will be working together to better evaluate those thoughts so that you can decide whether you really want to be guided by them. Does that make sense?

Clinicians may want to further stress the mood state dependency of thoughts and memories.

I think of emotions like sadness or depression as being like the theme music in a movie. In a movie, even though you may know that elements of the storyline are unlikely, the up-swell of the musical score can lull you into fully believing what you see on the screen. In the same way, a negative mood will help you remember other times in the past when you had the same emotion, and will bias your thinking to believe more negative thoughts (thoughts you know better than to believe when you are not depressed). In this way, your mood can influence your beliefs about the past and the present and future, making it feel like things did not work out for you in the past, and that things won't work out for you in the future. In treatment, we will work to help you treat your current depression-related thoughts as a mood-based guess about the world rather than a statement of reality, and help you to guide yourself more effectively in both what you think and do, so that you can undo some of the patterns that maintain depression.

Box 7.1 Academic Moment: A Cognitive-Behavioral Model of Depression

Major depression consists of symptoms including depressed mood, suicidal ideation, feelings of guilt or worthlessness, loss of interest and pleasure, sleep difficulties, fluctuations in weight, psychomotor irregularities, fatigue, concentration difficulties, and indecisiveness (*DSM-IV TR*; American Psychiatric Association [APA], 2000). Although there is some evidence for a genetic predisposition toward depression (Kendler et al., 1993), environmental factors (i.e., life events, coping skills) play a prominent role in the development and maintenance of major depression as well.

A cognitive-behavioral model of depression suggests that depression is maintained by a combination of negative dysfunctional thought processes and maladaptive behaviors that may be driven by such thought processes. More specifically, the cognitive conceptualization posits that depression is caused by distorted automatic thoughts, maladaptive assumptions, and negative schemas (Beck, 1967; Beck et al., 1979). Distorted automatic thoughts are often observed in a negative view of self (perceived as deficient, inadequate, or unworthy), the world (interactions with the environment are perceived as representing defeat or depriva-tion), and the future (current difficulties or suffering will continue indefinitely). Maladaptive assumptions are the guiding principles that underlie automatic thoughts and generally include "must," "should," or "if/then" statements. These rules of living (i.e., I must be liked by everyone; If I don't get all A's then I am a failure) are often rigid and impossible to live up to. Schemas represent maladaptive concepts of the self that are activated during periods of stress and reflect core beliefs about the self (i.e., I am unlovable) (Beck, 1967). The behavioral com-ponent of the model suggests that depression is a result of reinforcement for depressed behavior and a lack of reinforcement of more adaptive behavior (Ferster, 1973). In other words, depression is viewed as an absence of rewards or the inability to obtain rewards. Indeed, the decreased activity that is often observed among individuals with depression results in isolation from positive events. Therefore, inactivity significantly reduces access to reinforcing activities, allowing for an increased frequency and intensity of negative thoughts and depressed mood.

Effective CBT that is derived from the cognitive-behavioral model offers a combination of informational, cognitive restructuring, and behavioral activation interventions to bring about changes in depressive symptoms. Information on more comprehensive treatment protocols can be obtained from a variety of sources (e.g., Beck, 1995).

Cognitive restructuring can be focused at any of a number of levels of negative thoughts and beliefs. For example, changing the self-critical style ("Look at me, I can't do anything right") or a ruminative focus on the presence or meaning of symptoms ("They seem happy; how come I'm not happy?") represents one level for cognitive change. Also, changing the dysfunctional thinking styles (e.g., "Everyone must love me," "I can't make mistakes") and the core beliefs ("I am unlovable") that underlie them is an additional target of cognitive restructuring. The goal is to help the patient respond differently to these thoughts. Common negative thoughts are listed in Table 7.1 and on the Common Negative Thoughts in Depression handout in the appendix. Review of this table provides one means to help patients begin to attend to these thoughts not as the product of clear thinking, but as a symptom of depression.

A preparatory skill for cognitive restructuring is to instruct patients to "stop and listen in on" the sort of things they are saying to themselves. In particular, you want your patients to do this upon changes (either positive or negative) in mood. Cognitive restructuring strengthens the patient's belief that (1) thoughts can influence perfor-mance and (2) negative thoughts can increase depressive symptoms, which conse-quently interfere with functioning. In terms of a Socratic questioning style, the

Table 7.1 Common Negative Thoughts in Depression

- Negative thoughts about the self
  - I am a loser.
  - I am not lovable.
  - I am a failure.
- Negative thoughts about the future
  - I will never be happy.
  - Nothing will work out for me.
  - I will always be alone.
- Negative thoughts about the world
  - I will be rejected.
  - The deck is stacked against me.
  - Nothing good ever happens.

---

dialogue between clinician (C) and patient (P) in treatment may look like the following:

> **C:** When you feel depressed, what are your thoughts? What do you tell yourself?

Action:

Thoughts are written out for examination; written thoughts frequently look very different to patients than thoughts that are simply voiced.

> **C:** Now take a look at some of the thoughts you have listed. If anyone had thoughts like these, and believed them, how do you think that person would feel?

Action:

Elicit information about increased depressive mood due to negative thoughts.

> **C:** If anyone had thoughts like these, and believed them, what might the person do (or not do)?

Action:

Discuss with the patient how decreased activity contributes to the self-perpetuating nature of a depressive spiral.

One strategy for sensitizing patients to the feed-forward cycle of negative and self-critical thinking, particularly related to the symptoms of depression itself, is to use the following "Gargoyle" metaphor taken from Otto (2000). As will become evident, this metaphor is suitable only for patients without psychotic or delusional symptoms. The purpose is to help patients see their own self-critical responses to symptoms as part of the depressive process, and to mobilize their own efforts at finding an alternative to this pattern.

GARGOYLE METAPHOR

I would like to tell you how I think about depression, because I see it in terms of a powerful image. I view it as a heavy, stone gargoyle, and if I am depressed, I can feel the weight of it on my shoulder, making everything I do harder. It makes it harder for me to be motivated, harder for me to get anything done, harder to get out of bed, harder to concentrate. And one of the worst aspects of the gargoyle is that it isn't quiet. It is whispering in my ear. It is saying things like, "Look at you, you're depressed; what is the matter with you? You aren't happy like other people." In particular the depression gargoyle wants you to blame yourself, to remind you of other times in your life when things were going poorly, and to label everything that happens in extreme terms. If something does not go well, the gargoyle says, "you failed" or "you blew it" or "that was a disaster."

If you do something to get "back on track," the gargoyle will tell you that your attempts are useless. If you feel bad, the gargoyle will tell you that this is the way it will always be. If you make a mistake, the gargoyle will tell you that this occurred because you are flawed. This is the gargoyle's method. And remember, because you are depressed, many of the messages whispered by the gargoyle will feel true. The gargoyle tries to make everything appear darker, because if you blame yourself instead of the depression gargoyle, it can just keep sitting on your shoulder, weighing you down, making everything harder.

Now that is how I view depression. How does this perspective, this example of a depression gargoyle sound to you? Does it describe your depression at all?

By relabeling the source of thoughts as being depression (gargoyle) related, patients may better get distance on these thoughts. The metaphor serves as a memory aid for this new approach of viewing thoughts as emotion-driven and not necessarily accurate statements about the world or the self. After presentation, this metaphor should be discussed with the patient. If the patient finds it useful, clinicians may want to continue with the following:

If you would like, we can then use this gargoyle image when we talk about your depression. And in starting treatment for depression, the trick is to make sure you do not buy into the gargoyle's message. Over the next several weeks, I am going to ask you to listen for the gargoyle's voice in the way you talk to yourself. And when you hear this voice, I want you to label it as the voice of the "depression gargoyle."

As an alternative to this voice, I am going to ask you to adopt the sort of voice that I am using with you, a therapeutic voice—a voice that assumes that you are currently hurting, coming for help, need to have an ally, and need to treat yourself kindly while you are working at change. You need encouragement and support as you change patterns associated with depression. Don't let the gargoyle voice interfere with this process.

As we have emphasized elsewhere (Otto et al., 2009), when discussing the range of negative thoughts uttered by the gargoyle, you may want to include, "*The gargoyle may even be saying that therapy is useless, that there is no use in wasting the doctor's time.*" It is surprising how many patients will nod when their clinician introduces this thought. If this occurs, you may have identified a thought that is particularly hard for patient to introduce into the session. By voicing the thought and labeling it as the gargoyle's voice, you may have done much to stop the patient from accepting this particular dysfunctional thought.

Box 7.2 Academic Moment: Negative Thoughts

Experimental research on information-processing biases in depression has provided important insights into the correlates of negative automatic thoughts. For example, Bradley et al. (1997) observed that induced or naturally occurring sad mood elicited attention to negative words (e.g., hopeless) presented for long durations. Sloan et al. (2002) also found that dysphoric individuals have impaired interpersonal reactivity that is specific to happy faces, and other research has shown that depressed participants attend selectively to sad faces (Gotlib et al., 2004). These findings suggest that depression is characterized by slow, deliberate, and strategically directed attention to mood-congruent information. There is also strong evidence of a relatively enhanced memory for emotionally negative information in depression (e.g., Gilboa-Schechtman et al., 2002). Negative automatic thoughts in depression may then be reinforced by deliberate attention to, and memory for, negative information. By reducing the frequency and intensity of negative automatic thoughts with cognitive restructuring, information-processing biases that maintain symptoms of depression will also be reduced.

MONITORING THOUGHTS

A process of guided discovery is commonly used to help patients begin their cognitive restructuring. Self-monitoring of negative thoughts, where monitoring is linked to observed mood changes, is aided by the Thought Record provided in the Appendix of Forms and Handouts. An example of the review of the negative impact of a prototypic negative thought on mood follows.

> **P:** Yeah, I felt bad when sitting at dinner with my friends last night.
> **C:** Do you recall what specific emotion you were feeling at the time?

P: I was feeling sad.

C: What was going through your mind at the time?

P: What do you mean?

C: What were you thinking about when you were feeling sad?

P: I was looking at my friends and how happy they seemed; they must think I'm a loser.

C: What you just described is an automatic thought. These are thoughts that we are generally not aware of that pop into our heads from time to time. Everyone has automatic thoughts. However, they may lead to depression when the contents of the thoughts are distorted but we believe them to be true.

P: But what if they are true?

C: That is a good question. The first thing we have to do is teach you to identify these thoughts so you can better evaluate how true they are when they are happening.

P: How is that going to help me feel less depressed?

C: Well, how might your depressive symptoms change if you no longer believed your negative automatic thoughts to be true?

P: I suppose I might be less depressed.

C: OK, let's write this down so we can see how the process unfolds. When you have the thought, "I am a loser," you feel sad.

P: Right.

C: So it seems like what you are thinking (or telling yourself) influences the emotions that you have.

P: OK … I see.

IDENTIFYING COGNITIVE ERRORS

Negative thoughts can be especially hard to change when they are longstanding and mood congruent. When longstanding, thoughts begin to feel true simply because they have been rehearsed for so many years. They feel true because they are a habit. Likewise, negative thoughts can feel true because they are so congruent with a current mood state ("of course I am a bad person, because everything, include me, feels bad"). One use of the gargoyle metaphor is to put an alternative voice to these thoughts—helping patients identify them as feeling true only because of the depression gargoyle.

An alternative and more classic cognitive approach to challenging thoughts is to instruct patients to identify common cognitive errors in logic. Patients can then evaluate their thinking patterns in relation to these errors and, ideally, have an easier time challenging these thoughts when they know them to be an error. Classic errors were provided in Chapter 3 (Table 3.1) and are also provided in the appendix (see List of Cognitive Errors).

With this approach, patients are introduced to each error, and then asked, when discussing thoughts, to identify the error the thought represents. Challenging is part of a broader process of treating a thought as a hypothesis ("a guess about the world") and looking for evidence that supports or refutes the thought. An example of cognitive restructuring that emerged during a discussion of job opportunities follows:

> **P:** Yeah, I saw that the video rental store down the street from my apartment was hiring and I thought maybe I should apply.
>
> **C:** So what is stopping you?
>
> **P:** I don't know. I probably won't get the job.

Comment:

Notice that the patient is engaging in *fortunetelling* that is marked by pessimistic thinking. This cognitive style is extremely common in depression and it reinforces negative automatic thoughts about the self, world, and future. Importantly, this tendency to believe that things won't work out as you wish or that you won't get what you want can lead to a pervasive sense of hopelessness.

> **C:** So you are having the thought that you won't get the job?
>
> **P:** Yeah.
>
> **C:** If you believe that, what is the likelihood that you will apply for the job?
>
> **P:** Well, why even bother?
>
> **C:** And how does that make you feel?
>
> **P:** Hopeless, I guess.
>
> **C:** So, one consequence of not challenging the thought that you won't get the job is that you feel hopeless and more depressed?
>
> **P:** Yes.
>
> **C:** Well, what do you suppose are the chances of you getting the job if you don't apply for it?
>
> **P:** Well, I guess I'm certainly not going to get the job then.
>
> **C:** So it appears that another consequence of not challenging the thought that you won't get the job is that you don't apply for it, which guarantees that you don't get the job.
>
> **P:** Yeah, I see.

Comment:

Negative automatic thoughts, when unchallenged, often become self-fulfilling prophecies during the course of depression. Highlighting emergent observations of this process for each patient can improve treatment outcome. This information will provide the patient with a different context for better understanding "why bad things happen to me" and more importantly the role that their negative automatic thoughts play in the process. In the preceding example, the prediction that the patient won't get the job indirectly causes it to become true, by the very terms of the "prophecy" itself, due to functional contingencies between belief (I won't get the job) and behavior (no need to apply). This self-fulfilling prophecy then results in further depression that may result in a vicious downward spiral.

C: So what is your evidence that you won't get the job?

P: I don't know. I just *feel* like I won't get the job.

C: Hmm. You're not qualified for the job?

P: Well, I haven't looked at the qualifications yet.

Comment:

Notice that the clinician is indirectly providing the patient a "rational" context for evaluating the accuracy and utility of the negative automatic thought that he won't get the job. When one is evaluating the likelihood of getting a job, there are various "objective" criteria that one should consider. However, the patient provides an example of a negative automatic thought that is marked by emotional reasoning. Emotional reasoning consists of the patient thinking something must be true because he feels it so strongly. This strong conviction will result in discounting evidence that contradicts the negative automatic thought.

C: What do you imagine are some of the qualifications that would prevent you from getting the job?

P: I guess I really can't think of any.

C: So it sounds like when you get down to it, just *feeling* like you won't get the job is not very good evidence that you won't get the job.

P: I guess so.

C: So what is some evidence that you might be qualified for the job?

P: Oh, I don't know.

Comment:

Notice here that depressive symptoms may hinder the patient in generating positive self-statements or expectations. This is a common treatment "obstacle" for patients with depression. This obstacle can often be overcome by forcing patients to get "outside their own heads" and into the head of an objective third party.

C: If you were the manager of the video store, what qualifications might you look for in an employee?

P: I guess some previous experience?

C: Do you have any previous customer service experience?

P: I've never worked in a video store before, but I did used to work at a grocery store.

C: OK. What other qualifications might you look for if you were the boss?

P: Availability to work part-time hours?

C: Are you available?

P: Yes.

C: So is there good evidence that you are qualified for the job?

P: I guess so.

C: If there is good evidence that you are qualified for the job, how does that affect how you feel?

P: I guess I am feeling a bit more optimistic. It probably wouldn't hurt to at least apply for the job. But what if I don't get it? I don't know if I could handle that.

Comment:

A major aim of cognitive restructuring is to help patients to begin to engage in more adaptive self-talk and problem-solving strategies. This is done largely through challenging the accuracy and utility of negative automatic thoughts. However, as is clear from the latter portion of the preceding dialogue, the clinician must also prepare the patient to cope with negative outcomes. This is a good example of where focusing more on the *degree* of catastrophe may be more helpful for the patient than focusing on the *probability* of the negative outcome. For an event like not getting a job, it is more natural to focus on the degree of catastrophe given that the probability of a negative outcome may actually be quite high.

C: Well, there are no guarantees, and you certainly may not get the job. But you don't believe that you could cope with the disappointment of not getting the job?

P: Not really.

C: Well, not getting the job would be disappointing.

P: Yeah, I don't think I could handle another failure.

C: Hmmm... So it sounds like you are having the thought "I am a failure" when you think about what would happen if you did not get the job?

P: Yeah.

C: OK, now that we have identified the negative automatic thought, what is the next step?

P: Examine the evidence?

C: That's right. What is the evidence for it and what is the evidence against it?

P: I don't know. This one is tough.

C: Well, let's examine the thought. Let's imagine that you did not get the job and your interpretation of that one event is that you are a failure. How do you suppose you might feel?

P: It would not be good. I would be hopeless and probably say, the hell with it.

C: So when you say the hell with it, what would that mean?

P: I guess I would probably give up on getting a part-time job.

C: Hmmm… so accepting the thought that you are a failure is really going to affect how you cope with the possible outcome of not getting the job. In this case you feel helpless and give up trying.

Comment:

It is important to note the negative attributions which depressed patients make that will prevent them from being able to cope when negative events occur (which, of

---

Box 7.3 Academic Moment: Learned Helplessness

The learned helplessness theory posits that depression may result from lack of perceived control over external events (Seligman, 1975). This theory was derived from animal studies showing that animals exposed to uncontrollable shocks often show signs of depression. For instance, helpless animals often show both motivational (it takes them longer to initiate escape or avoidance responding) and cognitive (behavior not sensitive to environmental contingencies) deficits. Learned helplessness is viewed largely as a deficit in one's ability to learn a new response after being exposed to aversive stimuli that are perceived to be uncontrollable. In the context of depression, patients come to inaccurately believe, through learning history, that there is no relationship between their responses and environmental changes, and this impairs their motivation and ability to act in future situations where adaptive environmental changes are dependent on their responses (Maier & Seligman, 1976).

More contemporary views have identified individual differences in attributional style as an important moderator of the relationship between learned helplessness and depression (Abramson et al., 1978; Peterson & Seligman, 1984). Attribution styles are global/specific, stable/unstable, or internal/external in nature. Those prone to making *global attributions* believe that the cause of negative events is consistent across different situations. However, those prone to making *specific attributions* believe that the cause of a negative event is unique to a particular situation. *Stable attributions* are marked by beliefs that the cause of a negative event is consistent across time. Those prone to *unstable attributions* believe that the cause is specific to one point in time. Individuals who make *external attributions* assign causality to situational/external factors. However, those making *internal attributions* assign causality to factors within the person. Based on this attribution model, individuals who perceive negative events as global, stable, and internal are most likely to experience depression as a result of learned helplessness (Peterson et al., 1984).

course, they will). Accordingly, clinicians should help patients understand and accept that bad things do happen. This will also provide an opportunity to stress to patients that they do have control over their *response* to the occurrence of negative events. It is in this context of adaptive coping that depression can be reduced by preventing learned helplessness.

    P: Yeah.

    C: Hmmm... how does giving up help with your depression?

    P: I guess it doesn't.

    C: OK, so it sounds like the thought "I am a failure" if you did not get the job is not very useful when considering your symptoms.

    P: I get that, but that does not make it less true.

    C: OK, so we agree that the thought does not have very good utility, so let's think more about the accuracy of the thought. Is there any evidence that the thought "If I do not get the job, then I am a failure" might not be true?

[*The patient is silent.*]

    C: If a friend or family member applied for a job and did not get it, would that make them a failure?

    P: Well, I guess not.

    C: Hmmm... When someone wants to go about getting a job, how do they usually go about it?

    P: I guess most people just find jobs they like and start applying for them.

    C: OK, so most people apply for several jobs and they might not get some of them, right?

    P: Yes.

    C: Does that make them failures?

    P: No.

    C: In fact, not getting a job that one applies for is part of the process.

    P: OK, I see.

    C: So if you challenge the thought "I am a failure" if you don't get the job with a more rational way of thinking and realize that people apply for many jobs and they don't get all of them, how does that change your view of your ability to cope if you didn't get the job?

    P: Well, I really could use the money, so I guess I'll just have to find another part-time job to apply for.

Comment:

Challenging beliefs about one's ability to cope with a potentially negative event often provides patients with the crucial learning experience that how one copes with what actually happens may be a bigger determinant of depressive symptoms that the actual event itself. To empower patients with such tools in the context of a problem-solving approach to depression, patients should be encouraged to (1) select the most desirable solution, (2) develop a plan based on that solution, (3) schedule the first steps to implementing that solution, (4) evaluate the effectiveness of the solution, and (5) modify the solution as necessary.

BEHAVIORAL ACTIVATION

Behavioral activation (BA) aims to increase the frequency and quality of pleasant activities and consequently improve mood. BA increases activation systematically with graded exercises to increase the patient's contact with sources of reward. BA usually involves activity scheduling, ongoing monitoring of pleasant activities and feelings of mastery, and gradual exposure to challenging activities. As a procedure, BA involves five steps:

1. Provide a rationale
2. Monitor current activities
3. Identify potential activities
4. Develop activity hierarchy
5. Monitor progress

Box 7.4 Academic Moment: Behavioral Activation

The theoretical foundation for BA originates from traditional behavioral models of depression that posit that depression results from reinforcement of depressed behavior and a lack of reinforcement of more adaptive behavior (Ferster, 1973). Early investigations showed that basic BA strategies (i.e., pleasant event scheduling) were effective in treating depression. However, with the development of cognitive theory in the latter quarter of the 20th century, BA was viewed as insufficient, given the absence of a direct cognitive manipulation (Hopko et al., 2003). More traditional treatment approaches for depression consist of interventions that were traditionally regarded as purely "cognitive" and "behavioral" (Hollon, 2001). Although the efficacy of cognitive-behavioral therapies for depression is well documented, research has shown that behaviorally based manipulations alone can produce cognitive change.

Data from an initial study also found that BA may be equally effective for the treatment of depression as a comprehensive cognitive-behavioral intervention in terms of both overall treatment outcome and the alteration of negative thinking and dysfunctional attributional styles (Jacobson et al., 1996). This finding is consistent with the BA treatment rationale, which posits that changes in patterns of depressive behavior over time are likely to coincide with changes in depressive thoughts and mood, with change in thought and mood occurring as a consequence rather than a cause of behavior change. BA also appears to be equally effective as CBT in preventing relapse in depression (Gortner et al., 1998). A more recent study also found that BA was comparable in efficacy to antidepressant medication, and both significantly outperformed cognitive therapy among more severely depressed patients (Dimidjian et al., 2006). Extensions of this work have shown that BA may be as enduring as cognitive therapy with regards to relapse prevention and that both treatments are less expensive and longer-lasting alternatives to medication in the treatment of depression (Dobson et al., 2008).

Effective BA is derived from conceptualization of depression as a means of avoiding environmental circumstances that provide low levels of reinforcement (Jacobson et al., 2001). Thus, BA aims to extinguish avoidance behavior deemed central for maintaining symptoms of depression. By examining the consequences and function of depressed behavior and developing a context in which patients increasingly approach rather than avoid potentially rewarding situations, symptoms of depression may be efficiently reduced. Information on more comprehensive treatment protocols can be obtained from a variety of sources (e.g., Lejuez et al., 2001).

Providing a rationale

C: So it sounds like you have not been able to enjoy some of your former hobbies and social activities.

P: I just don't feel like doing much of anything.

C: Why do you think that is?

P: I don't know. I always feel tired and physically drained. Even little things seem to wear me out so I just don't want to do anything.

C: So due to your depression, you're always tired and don't presently feel as though you're able to get much done.

P: Yeah, that's right.

C: So once you are feeling better, do you think you will be more active and able to participate in the activities you used to enjoy?

P: I think so.

C: But getting yourself to feel better is much easier said than done, isn't it?

P: Yeah, it is.

C: Hmm. Maybe you need to become more active and put yourself into more positive situations in order to feel better. What do you think about that?

P: I don't know. Doing anything just seems so overwhelming.

C: I understand that it is difficult, but do you think you would feel better if you were able to find pleasure in the things you used to enjoy?

P: I guess so.

C: Do you think that if more positive experiences were associated with doing some of those things, they would become easier and easier to do?

P: Yes, I just don't know if I have the energy.

[*The patient appears reluctant.*]

C: Well, we will take it very slow and gradually work our way up through the activities that you will be doing for homework.

P: OK.

Monitoring current activities

C: Before we start, I would like to get a good sense of what your current activity level is. How have you been spending your days?

P: I'm not sure what you mean.

C: Well, tell me what your typical day is like.

P: There isn't much to tell, really. I'm not working, so my typical day is spent at home.

C: OK, what time do you typically get out of bed?

P: Well, lately I haven't been getting up until about 1 or 2 in the afternoon.

C: Then, what do you typically do after you manage to get up?

P: Sometimes taking a shower seems like too much work. So I might make my way over to the couch and watch TV for a while.

C: How long is "awhile"?

P: Well, I'm usually on the couch for most of the day.

C: That's a long time.

P: I don't sleep very well through the night. Even when I get out of bed at 1 or 2 in the afternoon, I don't feel rested. I feel sluggish and tired, so I often nap on the couch throughout the day.

C: Can you manage to do anything else?

P: Yeah, I get up from time to time to get a bite to eat, but even that's hard. I don't have much of an appetite anymore.

C: So you are not managing to do any activities during the day that could be potentially rewarding?

P: Not really.

C: Most of your day, then, is spent doing things that keep you depressed.

P: I guess.

C: Then how might things be different if you were doing more activities that were rewarding?

P: Well, I guess I might feel better.

Identifying potential activities

C: Let's spend a few minutes thinking about what activities you have time for and might enjoy.

P: OK.

[*Patient is silent.*]

C: What kind of activities did you used to enjoy?

P: [*Smiles*] I used to like working out.

C: How would you say that your depression differed when you were working out regularly?

P: [*Pauses*] I was feeling much better when I was working out. I used to run in the morning every other day at 7A.M.

C: So there is a relationship between your level of engagement in activities like working out and your level of depression?

Comment:

This dialogue exemplifies the importance of continuing to use the patient's own experience as supportive evidence for the rationale of BA. As a first step in a BA protocol, the clinician and patient must collaboratively determine the activities that need to be targeted. However, depressed patients may have some difficulty articulating activities that may be positively reinforcing. Developing a list of potentially pleasurable activities may be accomplished by asking about the patient's daily routine when he or she was not depressed. In this way, some pleasurable activities that are already in the patient's repertoire can be incorporated into the treatment program. This approach is more likely to increase mastery experiences that will also serve to improve the patient's mood. It may be beneficial for the clinician to suggest alternative pleasurable activities that are consistent with the patient's clinical presentation. Use the Pleasant Event List in the appendix to help determine these activities. The clinician and patient can review this list to select activities if the patient is unable to generate his or her own.

    P: You know, I used to love getting up in the morning to go for a run, and it felt pretty good to do it.

    C: That is important to keep in mind. If you are willing to slowly engage in this and other activities, you will find that your mood will improve.

    P: OK.

    C: Now let's make a list of about 11 other activities that you will have time for and might enjoy.

    P: I can list anything?

    C: Well, it is important to include activities that will bring a sense of pleasure or accomplishment.

    P: I see.

    C: Remember that activities that will bring a sense of accomplishment may not be easy. Also, when selecting activities, it is important to include things that can be observed and we can measure.

It is important to encourage patients to develop a list of activities that are tangible and measurable (e.g., go for a walk in the park twice per week) rather than those that are more abstract and cognitively oriented (e.g., think happier thoughts). Patients should be encouraged to develop a list of activities that vary in degree of difficulty. Limiting the list to very difficult activities may set the stage for failure and a delay of reinforcement. Table 7.2 shows a sample planned activity list.

Table 7.2 Sample Planned Activity List

Item	Activity	Level of Difficulty
1	Run every other day	10
2	Get up before noon	2
3	Go see a movie	3
4	Learn to play the piano	11
5	Clean out the garage	6
6	Get a haircut	1
7	Go on a date	8
8	Get a dog	7
9	Read a novel	5
10	Finish bachelor's degree	12
11	Go to church on Sunday	4
12	Paint the deck	9

Developing an activity hierarchy

C: Now that you have your list of 12 activities, rank them numerically from the least difficult to the most difficult.

P: OK.

[Patient ranks list; see Table 7.3]

C: So in looking at your list, getting a haircut is the least difficult thing to do and finishing your degree is the most difficult?

P: Yeah.

C: OK, now what we'll do is break down the activities into four levels with three activities in each level. So the first three ranked activities will be in the first level, the 4th through 6th activities will be in the second level, the 7th through 9th activities will be in the third level, and the 10th though 12th activities will be in the fourth level.

P: OK.

C: OK, your goal until I see you next time is to engage in all the activities in the first level. I realize that getting your hair cut may be a one-time activity until our next visit. However, getting up before noon is something you should try to do every day until we meet again. This week, you may want to try getting

Table 7.3 Sample Patient Hierarchy

Level 1
Get a haircut
Get up before noon
Go see a movie
Level 2
Go to church on Sunday
Read a novel
Clean out the garage
Level 3
Get a dog
Go on a date
Paint the deck
Level 4
Run every other day
Learn to play the piano
Finish bachelor's degree

up at 11.30 a.m. Then try getting up at 11 a.m. next week and then 10.30 a.m. the week after that.

Working through a hierarchy can help patients build momentum and a sense of stepwise success. As patients become more consistent in completing the activities in the first level, they should then move to the next, more difficult level of activities. Some of the activities may require the participation of family members. It may be helpful for patients to consider talking with family members and close friends about the goal of gradually increasing participation in rewarding activities and the role they can play in facilitating the accomplishment of that goal. For larger goals (level 3), the clinician may need to review component steps toward these larger goals, using the Steps to Goal Attainment form in the appendix.

Monitoring progress

C: OK, do you have any questions about how to complete the homework?

P: No. I think I can start to work on these three activities.

C: Very good. Part of the homework will consist of keeping track of the activities that you have done.

P: Keeping track?

C: Yes. This will help us monitor your progress. We can also assess if the activities are too hard or too easy so we can adjust them if we need to. It is important that you challenge yourself without becoming overwhelmed. Monitoring your progress will help us assess that.

P: How do I do that?

C: Well, I want you to get a notebook that lists the activities we have decided on. Each day I want you to put a *Y* next to an activity if you completed it and an *N* if you did not.

P: OK.

C: I also want you to write down the specific time of the day that you complete each task.

P: OK.

C: If you don't complete an activity assigned for homework due to unforeseen circumstances, we'll keep the activity on the list for you to do the next week. Does that sound OK?

P: I guess.

C: If you don't complete an activity because it is unreasonable or too difficult, we'll consider replacing that activity with one that is more ideal.

P: Sounds good.

SIGNS OF ADAPTIVE CHANGE

If treatment is progressing well, clinicians should be able to note a change in the way patients view their own thought content. Patients may spontaneously report the ability to "catch" negative thoughts when they are happening. Indeed, for many patients, cognitive restructuring "marches backward" in time: initial restructuring efforts occur on session days after the relevant event, subsequent cognitive restructuring occurs hours after the event with patients reviewing their thinking themselves, and finally it occurs in "real time," at the actual moment of the emotional event. As mood improves, so should problem-solving abilities (e.g., Williams et al., 2005), the ability to manage stress (Otto et al., 1997), and emotional reactivity to both positive and negative stimuli (e.g., Rottenberg, Gross & Gotlieb, 2005).

In providing CBT for depression, clinicians can think of themselves as promoting a three-step process of (1) engaging depressed patients in treatment, (2) helping them adopt a model of active cognitive restructuring and activity change in the face of negative affect, and (3) working to transition initial treatment gains into an *upward spiral* of positive affect, increasing problem solving, increasing activity, and more functional thinking patterns (Tang & DeRubeis, 1999). Indeed, when patients become fully engaged in active cognitive restructuring and activity completion, it is not unusual for them to have sudden, "I got it" experiences that reflect either a change in the way they react to dysfunctional thoughts or their return to productive and pleasurable activity. When these experiences are good, patients may suddenly improve between sessions; in fact, they may achieve half of their total treatment gains over the course of a week (Hopko, Robertson & Carvalho, 2009; Tang & DeRubeis, 1999). For example, in the treatment of depressed cancer patients who had received a brief (nine-session) BA treatment, 50% of patients reported a sudden reduction in depression (i.e., an average 11-point drop on the Beck Depression Inventory) between sessions (Hopko et al., 2009). Rather than representing a sign of a false improvement, sudden gains in therapy are predictive of maintained improvement over time (Hopko et al., 2009; Tang et al., 2007). As such, clinicians should be both vigilant for and supportive of sudden improvements in affect; these can represent real and reliable increases, and can occur in one third to one half of patients receiving CBT for depression.

8

CBT FOR GENERALIZED ANXIETY DISORDER

Placement of this chapter after those on panic disorder and depression is deliberate because CBT for generalized anxiety disorder (GAD) has commonalities with CBT for both these other conditions. Like panic and depression, GAD is characterized by a feed-forward cycle of negative affect and negative thoughts, with one influencing the other. There is typically no rapid escalation of the anxiety in this pattern to panic proportions, but the rapid interplay between anxiogenic thoughts and anxious feelings has clear commonalities with GAD. Likewise, the cognitive errors commonly present in panic disorder—overestimations in the probability of and degree of catastrophe of negative outcomes—are as common to GAD as to panic. Also, the ruminative quality of worry in GAD is reminiscent of that found in depression (enough so that DSM proscribes against diagnosing GAD for symptoms that occur strictly in the context of a major depressive episode), and cognitive restructuring efforts are similar for the two disorders.

CBT for GAD is directed toward breaking the patterns that maintain excessive anxiety and worry by teaching patients to (1) modify thinking patterns that promote anxiety and worry, (2) reduce anxious arousal, and (3) apply more effective coping strategies. To achieve these ends, CBT trains patients to respond differently to the cognitive, physical, and situational cues for excessive anxiety and worry. In the early stages of treatment, patients learn to identify triggers for worry and to modify catastrophic thinking, while also developing skills to encapsulate all-day worry into specific episodes. Later in treatment, patients learn relaxation techniques to reduce the physiological symptoms of anxiety that are associated with excessive worry. Final stages of treatment are aimed at eliminating avoidant thinking patterns, improving problem-solving skills, and enhancing the pursuit of valued activities.

INFORMATIONAL INTERVENTIONS

- Provide instruction about the nature of anxiogenic thoughts.
- Introduce cognitive strategies to reduce worry.
- Provide instruction in brief muscle relaxation.

CORE INTERVENTION ELEMENTS

- Assign monitoring of catastrophic thoughts with questioning of whether a more reasonable interpretation of events may exist.
- Review anxiogenic thoughts in session, with efforts to correct distortions in thoughts and overestimation of catastrophic outcomes in situations that trigger worry.
- Provide patient with a rationale for use of appropriate problem-solving strategies when faced with worry about routine events.
- Provide a "worry time" intervention to reduce the pervasiveness of worry.
- Provide overview of relaxation training strategies and instruct patient to practice these techniques to diminish anxiety.
- Complete worry exposures if needed.

INFORMATION: ORIENTING THE PATIENT TO CBT

Regardless of the style of informational intervention used, clinicians should make sure their patients understand the role of increased vigilance to and overestimation of the likelihood and impact of feared catastrophic outcomes in (1) engendering anxiety, (2) distracting the patient from the actual situation at hand, and (3) motivating cognitive and behavioral avoidance. You may wish to say something like the following:

> *To complement the medication treatment [or psychotherapy] I have been offering you, I am going to work with you to show you additional ways to manage your anxiety and to get back to living your life the way you want to. In particular, we are going to work together to reduce your worry and to increase your involvement in the activities that are important to you. To do that, I need to tell you more about some of the most common patterns in GAD.*
>
> *As you have likely noticed, worry usually takes the form of a "what if. . .?" question, and focuses on predicting something negative that might happen in the future. Although a small degree of worry can sometimes be useful to help us focus on and think through potential problems, the difference in GAD is that worry becomes the primary, automatic response to many different situations. In GAD worries also become repetitive; you may have noticed that you often worry about the same feared outcomes over and over again, as if this will help you "be prepared for the worst."*

When we worry, we sometimes predict or feel certain that something catastrophic will definitely happen, even though this outcome is only one of many possibilities. The emotions or physical sensations that tend to go along with this type of thinking are what we usually label as "anxiety." The physical symptoms that can be triggered with this type of worry and anxiety include things like restlessness, feeling keyed up or on edge, muscle tension, irritability, insomnia, and having trouble concentrating. Because we feel anxious, we don't stop to question the likelihood that the outcome we are afraid of will actually happen. There are also certain ways we behave that can happen as a consequence of excessive anxiety and worry, including procrastinating, checking things over and over again, perfectionism, and asking others for reassurance. It might seem like these behaviors and thinking decrease our anxiety in the short term, but they can actually end up helping anxiety persist in the long term because they serve as a way to avoid facing our real fears. Sometimes people think that the reason something catastrophic didn't happen is because we spent time worrying about it (and did things like double-checking and getting reassurance) in advance, but this serves to strengthen this dysfunctional pattern of worry and anxiety, and to worsen associated symptoms such as trouble sleeping and feeling restless and tense.

Box 8.1 Academic Moment: A Cognitive-Behavioral Model of GAD

In contrast to other anxiety disorders, in which there is a specific and relatively well-defined feared stimulus, GAD is characterized by chronic and diffuse anxiety in response to numerous internal and external stimuli. Research indicates that individuals with GAD worry about similar topics as do those without the disorder (e.g., family matters, work, finances, health-related problems) but that they experience their worry as less controllable and they worry more frequently, for a longer period of time, and about a greater number of topics (Borkovec, 1994). More recent investigations also suggest that individuals with GAD are more likely than non-anxious controls to worry about minor/routine matters such as time management and daily hassles (Roemer, Molina & Borkovec, 1997). Results from population-based twin studies suggest that the disorder is somewhat heritable (Hettema, Prescott & Kendler, 2001), and there is also some evidence for the role of early uncontrollable life events in creating a psychological vulnerability for the disorder (Malcarne & Hansdottir, 2001).

Cognitive-behavioral models suggest that individuals with GAD experience excessive anxiety and worry about everyday events because they fear potential catastrophic outcomes, particularly when faced with situations that are perceived as uncertain or uncontrollable (see Behar et al., 2009). Hypervigilance and other somatic sensations of anxiety develop as the body prepares to deal with possible future threats, and attention becomes focused on the individual's perceived inability to cope with unpredictable/uncontrollable events. This, in turn, increases anxious arousal and attention to threat-related stimuli. Indeed, studies comparing individuals with GAD to healthy participants suggests that patients show a pre-attentive bias to threat-related information, overestimate the likelihood of negative outcomes, and are more likely to interpret neutral or ambiguous stimuli as threatening (see MacLeod, 2004, for a review). Worry and other avoidance behaviors then develop as a way to cope with chronic anxiety and/or to escape from negative affect.

In support of the notion that worry serves as a motivated cognitive avoidance strategy for individuals with GAD, a number of studies by Borkovec and colleagues have shown that worry consists primarily of verbal linguistic thought rather than mental images of feared outcomes. Visual images are more emotionally evocative and are linked to increased autonomic arousal, whereas worry appears to dampen autonomic arousal (see Borkovec, Alcaine & Behar, 2004, for a review). Use of this strategy as the primary coping response to anxious arousal allows patients to avoid complete functional exposure to negative images, which disrupts emotional processing and perpetuates the anxiety associated with feared outcomes (Foa & Kozak, 1986). Research by Dugas and colleagues (1998) further suggests that patients with GAD show intolerance for uncertainty, overestimate the advantages of using worry as a coping strategy, and have little confidence in their ability to actively engage in problem solving.

As in panic disorder and social anxiety disorder, avoidant responses in GAD are reinforced because they decrease anxious arousal in the short term. In addition, worry about low-probability events (as is typical in GAD) is usually followed by their non-occurrence, which may lead to the superstitious belief that the act of worrying prevented the feared catastrophic outcome from happening.

In sum, a cognitive-behavioral model of GAD suggests that cognitive avoidance through worry (1) increases and maintains anxious apprehension, (2) prevents disconfirmation of rigidly held beliefs about feared catastrophic outcomes, (3) interferes with the emotional processing of feared outcomes, and (4) inhibits the application of more adaptive strategies such as problem solving. Accordingly, CBT protocols include a combination of education about the disorder, cognitive restructuring aimed at reducing worry about potential future threats and altering maladaptive interpretations of neutral stimuli as threatening, relaxation training aimed at reducing autonomic arousal and physical tension, behavioral interventions aimed at reducing avoidance behaviors, and problem-solving training aimed at increasing adaptive coping in the face of minor/routine matters. Results from numerous studies support the efficacy of CBT in reducing symptoms of GAD (see Hunot et al., 2007, for a recent meta-analysis). Information about fuller treatment protocols can be obtained from a variety of sources (e.g., Brown, O'Leary & Barlow, 2001; Dugas & Robichaud, 2006; Rygh & Sanderson, 2004; Zinbarg, Craske & Barlow, 2006).

ADDRESSING THE FORM AND CONTENT OF WORRIES

Cognitive interventions for GAD start with identification of the role and form of anxiogenic thoughts. This includes teaching patients about the "what if. . ." (feared consequence) form of these thoughts, as they may occur across life domains, including minor everyday matters ("What if I'm late for my appointment?"), family ("What if I leave my child with a babysitter? Something horrible will happen!"), finances ("What if I get behind on my rent and get evicted?"), work ("What if I don't get this project done perfectly? I'm going to get fired!"), and personal illness ("What if this headache is a sign of a brain tumor?"). As always, we recommend a mix of an instructional and Socratic approach in providing this information. Initial instruction, followed by self-monitoring (see the Thought Record and the list of Common Fears in Generalized Anxiety Disorder in the appendix, and also Table 8.1), provides the clinician with a chance to help patients see the consequences of this dysfunctional thinking style (*"Take a look at some of the thoughts you have listed [read to patient]. If anyone had thoughts like these, and believed these, how do you think that person would feel?"*) before progressing to cognitive restructuring.

Although the focus of these thoughts may be distributed across several different domains (e.g., harm befalling family members, financial or work problems, fears related to death and dying), the negative thoughts associated with GAD can be categorized broadly into two types of distortions: overestimations of the probability of negative outcomes, and overestimations of the degree of catastrophe of these outcomes.

In completing cognitive restructuring interventions, clinicians will need to decide whether to focus more on the probability of the negative outcome or its degree of catastrophe, or both. For feared events of low probability, like natural disasters or contracting a terminal illness, it is natural to focus on the probability of the event. For other events (e.g., being fired), focusing on the degree of catastrophe is more useful. Also, not infrequently patients may need to evaluate the cost of their continued fear

Table 8.1 Common Fears in Generalized Anxiety Disorder

- Fears of unpredictable or uncontrollable events
  - I couldn't handle it if I got sick.
  - If I don't worry about this, I'll be caught off guard by something horrible.
- Fears of failure
  - I am going to mess up on this project and lose my job.
  - If I don't get an A on the test, I'm going to fail this class.
- Fears of uncertainty
  - I can't handle not knowing how it will go.
  - I have to check just to make sure everything is OK.

---

versus the possibility of a truly bad outcome (e.g., fearing potential catastrophic outcomes on a daily basis and being hypervigilant to any signs of threat vs. "taking a chance" on this remote outcome and more fully engaging in life). When working with well-learned anxiogenic thoughts, the therapist does not instruct the patient to try to stop thinking this way. Rather, this dialogue is designed to help patients notice and then to question the helpfulness or accuracy of their thought process. This lays the groundwork for the introduction of more adaptive alternative cognitive responses when faced with worry triggers. This type of dialogue may also be helpful to explore the patient's positive beliefs about the function of worry.

As with cognitive restructuring for other anxiety disorders, we think it is useful to help patients develop an ability to "marvel" at the degree of negativity of their thoughts. This is done to gain emotional perspective on these thoughts and their function (e.g., "Ouch, listen to what I am saying to myself; these are really negative scary thoughts. Do I really want to keep coaching myself that way?" or "It is really hard on me to keep thinking this way; these thoughts could keep *anyone* scared and vigilant—that is, if they believe them").

In the session, cognitive restructuring is started by helping patients identify specific thoughts in specific situations.

> **C:** So you told me that you worry a lot when your boss comes over to your desk to ask about a project. That seems to be a real trigger for you. Can you tell me more about what you are afraid will happen in this situation?
>
> **P:** When she comes over I'm wondering if I did something wrong. . . . I mean, why would she check on me unless I made a mistake?
>
> **C:** [Despite this logical error, the clinician chooses to focus on the catastrophizing.] And what would be so bad about it if you did make a mistake?
>
> **P:** Well, if I made a mistake then I'm pretty sure she is thinking that I'm incompetent and that she is going to fire me. So I worry all the time that she's going to come up and tell me to pack my things and go. I can't concentrate on my work because I'm so worried about it.
>
> **C:** So having your boss come over automatically triggers the thought "I must have made a mistake and now I'm going to be fired." It sounds like you are focusing on the worst possible outcome in this situation.
>
> **P:** That's right. I know it might sound ridiculous, but it is on my mind all the time. As soon as I see her coming my way I start to feel really nervous and I lose track of what I am doing.

Notice that in this example the patient makes a catastrophic interpretation ("I'm going to lose my job") in response to a neutral stimulus (the boss stopping by).

Once the clinician has helped the patient to describe the nature of the feared outcome, he or she can choose to focus on helping the patient evaluate the probability of the feared outcome as well as the patient's ability to cope should this outcome occur ("decatastrophizing" the feared outcome). During this process the patient is prompted to recognize the presence of coping abilities even in the face of a worst-case scenario. To help patients decide if they can actually cope with the event, should it occur, the clinician asks questions such as:

- And could you cope with that if it actually happened?
- Have you ever had something like that happen before?
- If you saw that happen to someone else, what would you think (do)?

Clinicians need to make sure that they do not ask these questions until the patient gets very specific about what he or she fears happening. In other words, it makes far less sense to ask the question about global negative descriptors (e.g., "And could you cope with something simply horrible?") than a specific outcome (e.g., "And could you cope with losing your job?").

PROBLEM-SOLVING TRAINING

Individuals with GAD often have difficulty solving everyday problems, mostly due to low levels of confidence in their ability to cope effectively with routine stressors. They may have negative beliefs that manifest in failing to recognize problems before it is too late to engage in problem solving, finding it unusual to have a problem, and seeing problems as threats to be avoided rather than as challenges to be embraced.

To help patients cope more effectively with their problems, it is useful to help them categorize their worries into (1) those that are related to concrete problems that can be solved in the near future or (2) those that pertain to improbable or imagined catastrophic outcomes that may or may not occur at some indeterminable point in the future (see van der Heiden & ten Broeke, 2009). The former are termed "productive worry" and can be the target of problem-solving training interventions (see the Problem-Solving Worksheet in the appendix), while the latter are referred to as "unproductive worry." As noted, worry exposure (described in the sections that follow) is assigned to help manage the anxiety associated with unproductive worry.

GAINING CONTROL OVER CHRONIC UNPRODUCTIVE WORRY

Unlike many of the other anxiety disorders, where anticipatory anxiety and phobic responses are linked with discrete cues, worry may become a chronic, all-encompassing event that takes over the lives of patients with GAD. Because of the free-floating nature of worry, clinicians may need to devote effort to constraining worry into discrete episodes where it can become the focus of other techniques, including the effects of repetitive exposure (Borkovec, Wilkinson, Folensbee, & Lerman, 1983; van der Heiden & ten Broeke, 2009). *Worry time* is a strategy for achieving this goal. With the worry time intervention, patients are asked to save all of their worries for a specific worry time each day. This worry time is often scheduled for the early evening, after work. Consistent with the goal of using worry time to constrain the environmental and time cues for worry, it should occur outside the bedroom and family room, and should preferably occur at a desk in a room or space reserved for work tasks. During worry time patients are to write out their primary concerns, then allow themselves to think constructively about the worry for approximately 45 minutes. Patients are to end worry time with relaxation practice and then "save up" their worries for the next 23 hours until the next worry time. Clinicians should instruct patients to take their worry time seriously, and truly defer all worries (taking notes if necessary to be able to rekindle a worry at the appointed time) until the specific worry time. Also, clinicians may need to explain that this method is to be used for recurrent worries, not the typical problems that come up over the course of a day and need immediate attention. If worries are actually problems in need of novel solutions, problem-solving procedures should be taught as per Chapter 5.

The expectation for the worry time intervention is that patients tend to become bored or annoyed with both their worries and their worry time after 10 to 15 days of repetition. It is not uncommon for a patient to exclaim, "But I don't need to worry about these things; it's a waste of time." This is one of the desired effects of the intervention: to focus enough useful thinking on repetitive worries that anxiety in response to these thoughts diminishes. Asking patients to write out these worries facilitates this process by slowing down and making explicit the thought processes underlying anxiety. As such, worry time is a form of exposure. It breaks up the usual mechanism of worry (often a rapid flitting from one worry concern to another) and has patients focus with clarity on individual worries in a planned way. Also, worry time helps clear out worry during the remainder of the day, and as chronic worry diminishes patients are likely approaching their worry time with less anxiety and a clearer head. If the worry time intervention works particularly well, patients may note that they have extra time during the day to think about other things. This would be an excellent time to discuss pleasant event planning as per the previous chapter.

PROCEEDING FROM WORRY TIMES TO FORMAL WORRY EXPOSURES

As noted, worry time is a form of exposure provided by the systematic re-introduction and examination of specific worry concerns. The use of a paper and pen to write out the worries slows down the worry process, helping ensure that worries are attended to in a new (and often more objective) way than is typical for the patient. Clinicians should also review worry topics with patients to judge whether any should be the target of problem-solving efforts (see Chapter 5). If worries are not appropriate for problem solving, and if worry exposure has not decreased the salience of specific worries, additional and more direct exposure procedures should be considered. These exposure procedures take more session time; hence, we introduce them here as a secondary strategy to worry time interventions. Also, we start with a briefer version of worry exposure: exposure to individual anxiogenic statements.

In the brief version, a specific worry is targeted for repetition, with the goal of sapping the emotional power of that particular concern. This procedures relies on the assumption that with repetition of a statement over and over again (i.e., 20 times), the meaning and salience of that statement changes. Elsewhere, we have detailed this procedure for specific negative thoughts that may be slow to change in the treatment of social anxiety disorder, such as "I am a failure" (Hofmann & Otto, 2008, pp. 116–118). Here, the clinician identifies a thought that is particularly anxiogenic and has been resistant to change with logical analysis (e.g., "something will happen to the kids if they are left home with a babysitter"). The patient is then to repeat this thought aloud in session, speaking it forcefully, and at times almost theatrically, for 20 repetitions. To prepare for this exposure, the clinician instructs patients to observe their emotional responses as they have a chance to focus on their feared thought.

> **C:** This thought "something will happen to the kids if they are left home with a babysitter" has been particularly troubling for you. You have repeated it to yourself so many times, and it has been accompanied by so much anxiety, that it serves as an automatic cue for feelings of dread and further worry. Also, because you have said it to yourself so many times, it seems like it just feels true, so much so that you are having some trouble evaluating whether it is an accurate thought.
>
> **P:** Yes, it just sets me off; I don't want the kids to get hurt. It feels so true.
>
> **C:** Yes, and because it feels so true, I have a procedure that I would like you to try that may change the feeling of this thought. I am going to ask you to repeat this thought over and over again, 20 times. I want you to say it aloud, and I want you to say it with some vigor. And, I want you to notice how it feels to say it in this way, over and over again for 20 times.
>
> **P:** Oooh, I don't like the idea of that; usually I kind of want to push that thought away.
>
> **C:** Well, then this will be an interesting experiment for you, to see what it is like to really focus on the thought over and over again. Are you ready to try?

P: OK. Something will happen to the kids if they are left home with a babysitter.

C: Good, again, but a bit louder.

P: Something will happen to the kids if they are left home with a babysitter.

C: Good, again.

P: Something will happen to the kids if they are left home with a babysitter. This is weird. [*The patient completes 10 more repetitions.*] This is weird. It sounds so stupid.

C: It is odd. Keep going—you have 7 more.

P: [*Patient continues*] This is odd. The thought started to sound almost stupid. I mean, the kids *are* with a babysitter.

C: Yes, it is a thought that has plagued you for some time and has way too much access to your emotions. You just got your first chance to develop some distance from that thought. Here, let me write it out for you in black and white. Take a look at that thought, and look at it for what it is—it is a thought that has terrorized you. It is time you take the emotional power away from this thought. Take a good look at it, and then I would like you to do the 20 repetitions aloud again.

If the patient responds well to this in-session exposure, then the clinician will want to assign home practice. For home practice, the patient is to take a copy of the written statement and complete 20 exposures. This is preferably done when the patient is not in the middle of a worry episode, and should be preceded by a review of the rationale for the procedure: "This is a thought that has way too much influence in my life; I am going to sap some of its emotional power."

Fuller CBT programs for GAD also emphasize prolonged worry exposure procedures (e.g., Zinbarg et al., 1993; van der Heiden & ten Broeke, 2009). For these procedures, our preference is to instruct patients in a *CEO thinking* approach (see Chapter 3) of more mindfully observing the products of their own mind. The goal of these procedures is to try to lessen the emotional salience of a fuller catastrophic image by having patients hold that image in their minds. Self-instruction might include the following:

Here is a frightening image that has been motivating my worry. I am going to get used to having an image like this pass through my mind without having to react to it with anxiety and worry. It is not a pleasant image, nor is it a true image, but it is an image I can get used to so that it can't push me around.

With this instructional framework, the patient is then to hold a single worry-based image in mind for 20 to 30 minutes (returning to the image should it begin to slip away) while also being aware of other thoughts and feelings. These procedures naturally have the element of exposure to anxiety sensations, and again, familiarity with Chapter 6 (treatment of panic disorder) can help clinicians promote comfort with these sensations (e.g., "Feeling anxious does not mean my thoughts are true or that I have to worry about something; it is just a feeling").

Again, these procedures are more intensive and require careful attention by the clinician to how the patient is reacting to his or her anxiety, and whether safety behaviors (see Chapters 4 and 6) are being used. Hence, in terms of ordering this intervention, use of more standard cognitive, worry time, and relaxation procedures may be selected as initial strategies if fuller session time cannot be devoted to persistent worries. The goal is to use worry exposure to help patients become more comfortable with the emotional distress that accompanies certain images, instead of employing worry as a cognitive strategy to avoid this level of distress.

As a procedure, worry exposure involves six steps:

1. Providing the rationale for exposure and identifying emotionally distressing images that trigger worry for the patient
2. Creating a hierarchy of feared and avoided images by ranking the extent to which each image provokes anxiety or distress for the patient
3. Eliciting a detailed narrative of each image from the patient. The patient is instructed to describe the image in as vivid detail as possible, using all of his or her senses
4. Helping the patient not to engage in cognitive avoidance during the exposure, and instructing the patient to pay attention to the actual emotional distress provoked by the image
5. Repeating steps 3 and 4 until the patient's distress level is reduced by half. If possible, it can be helpful to create an audio recording of the narrative for the patient to play back during repeated exposures
6. Discussing what was learned from the exposure, with attention to having the patient evaluate changes in the believability (degree of likelihood and degree of catastrophe) of the anxiogenic image, changes in the intensity of the evoked anxiety, and changes in the belief in alternative outcomes

Formal worry exposure is typically initiated with an image that provokes a moderate amount of distress for the patient. The goal of repeated exposures is to first help patients become comfortable with the feared images in the clinician's office. After the clinician has modeled the procedure in the office, additional practice can be assigned for the patient to complete at home. The following example assumes that the patient has already identified several images that trigger worry, and that worry time procedures, despite consistent use, have not decreased the salience of these select images.

C: Today we are going to work on a technique called worry exposure. This means focusing on, rather than avoiding or worrying about, images that you find distressing. When people are repeatedly exposed to images that they find upsetting, the images are no longer as anxiety provoking. In many ways, it is like watching a horror movie over and over again until you get bored—the images lose the ability to frighten you. Do you have your list of imagery situations with you today?

P: I brought it in, but I'm not so sure I want to think about these things. I'm already thinking about these things all the time!

C: I'm glad you brought this up. You are worrying a lot about bad things that could happen, and this can feel like an active process. But worry actually keeps you from experiencing the discomfort that comes along with these images and learning that it will dissipate on its own. And that is exactly why I want you to have some practice facing these images today.

P: OK.

C: We're going to start with the image on your list that you think will provoke only moderate distress. It looks like you listed being at work and having the boss come over to tell you that you are fired.

P: Yeah, that one is pretty strong. Since we talked it through last time I'm not quite as upset by it, but I still don't like to imagine it.

C: So what I want you to do now is to close your eyes and describe to me in as much detail as possible and as vividly as you can what this scenario would be like. It is best if you describe the situation as though it is happening to you right now, right here. Try to use all of your senses and describe to me where you are, what you see, how you feel, and what thoughts you are having.

    A few other things before we get going. If you start to feel uncomfortable and want to avoid this image, I will help you to stick with it. We will also make an audio recording of this story [*e.g., with a digital recorder*] so that you can take it home and listen to it. From time to time I will ask you for your distress level on a 1-to-100 scale. Please answer quickly and try not to leave the image. When you finish the story, I will ask you to start over again from the beginning, without pausing. This is to help you become accustomed to focusing on, rather than using worry to escape from, these distressing images. We will have some time at the end to talk about your experience with the exposure. Do you have any questions before we start?

P: I don't think so.

C: And how would you rate your level of distress right now?

P: I guess it is about a 50.

[*Clinician starts recording.*]

C: OK, let's get started. Now close your eyes and picture yourself sitting at your desk. Imagine what it feels like and describe to me what is happening as vividly as you can.

P: Right, so I'm at my desk and I've got a whole bunch of spreadsheets in front of me and I know that I need to have the budget ready for a meeting with my boss in a few minutes. I'm thinking to myself that I'm behind schedule and I'll never get it all done in time. I can feel my neck and shoulders getting all tense and the room is looking a little fuzzy around me. Then out of the corner of my eye I can see my boss coming down the hall towards my cubicle. I start to panic a bit, thinking that I'm not prepared for this meeting and she's going to know that I'm no good at my job. . . she's probably been waiting for any excuse to fire me and now I'm giving it to her. I really hate imagining this.

C: You are doing great. Just stick with the image and tell me what happens next.

Comment:

The patient is tempted to employ cognitive avoidance strategies. At these moments it is helpful for the clinician to encourage the patient by using statements such as, "You are doing fine, just stay with the image," "I know this is difficult. You are doing a great job; stay with your feelings."

P: My heart is pounding and I can feel my throat getting all dry. She comes into my cubicle and I can barely manage to say hello. It is just awful. And then she starts to say "I'm sorry to spring this on you right before our meeting, but there's something we need to discuss. It is about your performance. You just haven't been meeting our milestones and I'm afraid we're going to have to let you go." Now I'm really just freaking out. I feel all sweaty and like I might pass out. My hands are shaking and I can barely focus enough to throw some of my things into a box. I'm wondering if they are going to have the security guard escort me out and then everyone will know I got fired and I'm a failure. All I can think about is how we won't have enough money to survive and I've let my family down. I can't stop thinking this way. Pretty soon we'll lose our house, I'll be out on the streets, and my wife and kids will leave me. I'll end up alone and miserable. It is so awful!

C: What is your level of distress now?

P: A 60, maybe 65.

C: Now I want you to start again from the beginning, providing as much detail as possible and sticking with the image without trying to distract yourself in any way.

P: OK, so I'm sitting at my desk at work with all my spreadsheets in front of me...

[*Narrative continues*]

Comment:
The clinician should have the patient repeat this narrative until the patient's rating of distress is cut in half (in this case imaginal exposure would be terminated when the patient's peak distress rating falls to about 30). The clinician then discusses what the patient noticed during the exposure and what was learned from the experience. This discussion may be relatively brief, but it is important for the clinician to reflect on the fact that the patient was able to tolerate the emotional distress triggered by the image and that this emotional response diminished after repeated exposures.

C: Great work. What did you notice as we went through this exercise?

P: Well, it was really hard at first. I didn't want to picture losing my job and all the terrible things that would happen. But it was strange: when you had me tell the story again, it didn't bother me as much.

C: So you found that the amount of distress associated with this image went down when you faced the fear rather than distracting yourself.

P: Yeah, I was surprised about that because I never would have done this on my own. I told myself I just couldn't handle it. Maybe I just wasn't giving myself a chance.

C: That is exactly the goal of exposure. You will find that the more you allow yourself to picture the feared outcome, the less it will bother you.

Comment:
The goal of repeated exposures is to first help patients get comfortable with the feared images in the clinician's office, and to then practice these exposures at home. For example, following the preceding dialogue, the clinician may say:

C: OK, your goal until I see you next time is to imagine these scenarios daily, trying to get bored with the images so that your reaction to your worry triggers is more automatically, "Big deal. I've pictured this before. I don't have to worry about it."

Comment:
Depending on the nature of the anxiogenic image, exposure is sometimes aimed at reducing emotional arousal to a level sufficient to allow effective evaluation and problem solving. The patient does not get inured to outcomes such as job loss, but does get enough emotional distance from this recurrent image to better engage in relevant problem solving or job tasks related to actual job success. In other words,

by removing a chronic "false alarm" anxiety signal, the patient is better able to attend to relevant problem-solving behaviors in life.

RELAXATION TRAINING

Relaxation training is a longstanding and efficacious intervention for GAD. Progressive muscle relaxation exercises provide the patient with a useful tool for targeting chronic anxious arousal. This technique is reviewed in Chapter 5. In assigning any home practice, it is important for the clinician to check in regularly on whether the intervention was completed and whether it was effective for its target symptom. This active review will help link relaxation to the overall efforts provided by the clinician.

SIGNS OF ADAPTIVE CHANGE

If treatment is progressing well, clinicians may notice patients becoming increasingly annoyed with their own worry patterns. The sense that worry is protective will fade, and patients may spontaneously report frustration at both the form ("Look how extreme that is") and content ("I just don't need to worry about *that* again") of their thoughts.

Other patients may realize benefit through initial changes in anxious arousal brought by relaxation training. These patients may start to notice the state-dependency of their negative thoughts ("You know, when I'm less anxious, I am so much less bothered by some of these thoughts"). This change can then be applied to renewed cognitive interventions to help to solidify this change in reactions to negative thoughts.

9

CBT FOR SOCIAL ANXIETY DISORDER

CBT is directed toward breaking the patterns of fear and avoidance of social and performance situations by helping individuals (1) learn that social demands and social errors are less dire than imagined and (2) relearn, and in some cases learn, a sense of safety in avoided social and performance situations. To achieve these ends, CBT provides patients with training to re-evaluate and react differently to the somatic, cognitive, and situational cues for social fears and avoidance. In the early stages of treatment, patients learn that their self-imposed social and performance expectations usually exceed those that others have for them, and that they attend to minor social mishaps to a far greater extent than do those around them. Exposure training helps patients learn the distinction between their fears of failure in social interactions and actual objective levels of social performance; by learning that their goals are routinely met in social situations, patients' anxiety begins to dissipate. In addition, patients get direct experiences with tolerating minor social errors and re-evaluating the consequences of these errors. The final stages of treatment are aimed at eliminating avoidant patterns and enhancing the pursuit of valued activities. When these steps are completed, patients tend to achieve long-term relief from social anxiety disorder.

INFORMATIONAL INTERVENTIONS

- Provide information on the role of catastrophic thoughts in social anxiety, and help patients learn about excessive expectations for social perfection and the belief that others will focus on and respond derisively to their minor social mishaps or anxiety-related symptoms.
- Provide instruction in stepwise exposure to avoided social situations.

CORE INTERVENTION ELEMENTS

- Assign monitoring of negative and self-critical thoughts, including catastrophic interpretations of the meaning of social errors or social anxiety symptoms.
- Review these thoughts, and efforts to correct distortions in thoughts, during sessions.
- Provide the patient with an opportunity to present and process a 3-minute presentation in session with you, to learn he or she can achieve goals of the presentation even if anxiety is present (i.e., anxiety does not equal failure).
- Provide instruction in strategies for stepwise exposure to avoided social situations; assign exposures.
- Instruct patients in exposure to social mishaps; assign exposures.
- Monitor exposure progress in follow-up visits.

A MODEL OF THE DISORDER AND ITS TREATMENT

A great deal of data supports a cognitive-behavioral model of social anxiety disorder (see, for example, Clark & McManus, 2002). Some of this information is summarized in Figure 9.1, which depicts a feed-forward cycle between expectations of poor performance, vigilance to minor errors and symptoms, rising anxiety and urges to avoid, and the maintenance of negative self-evaluations based on escape and avoidance of social performance situations. Absent from the model is actual impairment in social skills, based on the notion that the majority of patients with social anxiety disorder suffer not from the absence of social skills, but from inhibition in the use of the skills they do have (Heimberg, 2001). For patients who display actual skill deficits despite exposure practice (e.g., those who do not have the skills to complete social interactions when anxiety is not an issue), referral for active training in social skills is warranted.

One characteristic of current CBT protocols for social anxiety disorder is the rehearsal of social performance in the context of social cues. This is one reason for the popularity of a group treatment format for social anxiety disorder (e.g., Hope, Heimberg & Turk, 2006): the treatment group provides the social setting for exposure rehearsals. Because of the number of patients who need to complete exposure practices as part of in-session treatment, these group meetings can be quite long (e.g., over 2-hour sessions). Obviously, such long protocol-based treatment does not fit in the brief-session format of component interventions stressed in this book. Nonetheless, it is useful to ask what is provided and what is learned in these longer group sessions, and what principles and procedures can then be offered in a briefer, individual component treatment approach.

In Heimberg's CBT for social anxiety disorder (Hope et al., 2006), for example, cognitive and exposure interventions are combined so that anxiogenic thoughts and

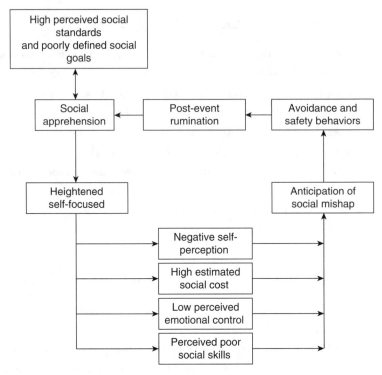

Figure 9.1 CBT Model of Social Anxiety Disorder
(Reprinted from Hofmann, S. G. (2007). Cognitive factors that maintain social anxiety disorder: A comprehensive model and its treatment implications. *Cognitive Behavior Therapy*, Vol 36:4, pp. 195–209, Taylor & Francis Ltd.)

their alternatives are examined in the context of exposure. Prior to exposure, patients receive training in identifying cognitive distortions characteristic of social anxiety disorder ("I will blow this talk; everyone will think I'm a fool") and in formulating more rational responses to these fears ("Even if I'm anxious, I'm probably going to be able to say several important things about the topic I'm presenting in front of this group"). Patients then complete exposures in front of the group (e.g., give a brief talk), and have the opportunity during the exposure to confront their anxiogenic thoughts ("I'm going to blow this talk"), provide rational responses to these thoughts ("I will likely make my core points"), assess their actual level of anxiety during the presentation, and evaluate, after completing the exposure, whether the objective goals for the presentation were met. These objective goals explicitly do not include "not be anxious" but instead are focused on the social performance (e.g., "Keep talking for at least 3 minutes, and communicate two core points about my topic"). When a group is not readily available, clinicians can arrange for others (e.g., members of clinic staff) to join the session for a few minutes as an audience for brief exposures, or may use videotaped performances so that a talk is a "public" event (the videotape also allows for objective review of actual performance with the patient).

From such exposure procedures, patients are provided with the chance to learn the following: (1) the difference between their negative or catastrophic expectations and their actual social performance (i.e., they did not actually freeze up or "blow it"), (2) the difference between their level of anxiety and their achievement (i.e., that social goals tend to be met despite the presence of anxiety), (3) that anxiety has a specific pattern and is often not high consistently during the talk (e.g., their anxiety may peak during the 20 seconds before and the first 20 seconds after the start of the presentation, and then decrease later), (4) that there may be a link between attending to the catastrophic thought and peaks in the anxiety, (5) that social errors or evidence of anxiety in social situations do not have the expected catastrophic consequences, and (6) that their self-expectations and self-evaluations tend to be hyper-critical, especially in relation to success as defined by the objective goals that were structured prior to the exposure. Any one of these learning outcomes may be important for a given patient's pattern of social phobia, and different protocols of treatment have been devised to better target one or another of these learning goals. For example, Hofmann and Otto (2009) have stressed the importance of challenging inflated estimates of the emotional and social costs of social errors by using programmed exposure to social mishaps.

For brief component treatment, clinicians should target these social- and performance-related outcomes using a combination of informational, cognitive, and exposure procedures that can be best provided within the clinician's practice environment. Outlined here are minimal component interventions for this task.

INFORMATIONAL INTERVENTIONS

The goal of these interventions is to help the patient identify elements of the ongoing cascade of anxiogenic thoughts, anxiety, and avoidance that characterize social anxiety disorder. Figure 9.1 provides an illustration of these elements (see also the figure in the appendix).

Regardless of the style of informational intervention used, clinicians should make sure their patients understand the role of increased vigilance to and overestimation of the likelihood and impact of social mishaps and anxiety symptoms in (1) enhancing anticipatory anxiety, (2) distracting the patient from the social or performance task, and (3) motivating avoidance. It is important to remember that these catastrophic misinterpretations are one component of the core fears of social anxiety; the model includes helping patients understand that avoidance only further heightens anxiety and impairs function. Overall, overestimated fears of failure, embarrassment, or humiliation in social and performance situations are introduced as a set of cognitions that place individuals at risk for increased anxiety and avoidance, and alongside avoidance help maintain the disorder once established (see Academic Moment, Box 9.1).

Box 9.1 Academic Moment: A Cognitive-Behavioral Model of Social Phobia

According to a cognitive-behavioral model of social anxiety disorder, the characteristic way in which individuals process social information from their environment contributes to the development and maintenance of social anxiety. Specifically, individuals with social anxiety disorder produce distorted mental representations of how they appear to others. Such mental representations are based partially on memory, internal cues (i.e., somatic sensations), and external cues (i.e., facial display of others). The mental representations of the self that emerge during anxiety-provoking social situations often reflect excessive self-focused attention. Indeed, research has shown that there is a bias for individuals with social phobia to interpret ambiguous social information in a more negative manner when the information is processed in relation to themselves (Amir, Foa & Coles, 1998).

Maladaptive assumptions that are driven by excessively high standards for performance, expectations of perfection, and/or excessive need for approval also underlie social phobia. Such processes may represent higher-order psychological vulnerabilities. This psychological vulnerability then increases the likelihood of socially relevant negative automatic thoughts (i.e., "I'm a loser," "They think I'm a fool," "I'll say something stupid") that are self-focused in nature. These negative automatic thoughts also motivate individuals with social phobia to be hypervigilant for signs of disapproval from others (e.g., frowns, expressions of anger or disgust). They are also hypervigilant for aspects of their own social behavior that may elicit negative evaluations from others (e.g., stuttered speech). One consequence of this "multitasking" in social situations is that it may actually increase the probability of a disruption or feared mishap in performance during social situations (MacLeod & Mathews, 1991).

As noted in Figure 9.1, increased self/other-focused attention during social situations elicits anxiety, and vice versa. The commonly reported symptoms of anxiety when in social situations include palpitations, trembling, sweating, tense muscles, dry throat, blushing, and headaches. For some patients, anxiety symptoms may reach the level of a full-blown panic attack. These symptoms themselves often become additional sources of focus, embarrassment, and distress for individuals with social phobia. In a recent study, high-blushing individuals showed significantly greater levels of social anxiety in a self-focused attention task compared to low-blushing individuals (Zou, Hudson & Rapee, 2007).

The fear of experiencing anxiety symptoms and of negative social and performance evaluation ultimately leads to passive avoidance (not making eye contact) and active avoidance (not attending social functions) as well as the use of various cognitive and behavioral strategies designed to prevent feared catastrophes from occurring during social interactions. For example, patients with social phobia may attempt to memorize everything they plan to say during a conversation to avoid appearing incompetent. Avoidance and the use of safety behaviors maintain maladaptive assumptions, because if the feared catastrophe does not happen the nonoccurrence is attributed to avoidance and safety-seeking behaviors.

The cognitive-behavioral model of social phobia suggests that avoidance and safety behaviors (1) increase anxiety symptoms, (2) prevent disconfirmation of unrealistic beliefs about feared social consequences, and (3) maintain self-attention, using processing capacity that could otherwise be used to disconfirm maladaptive thoughts (or to attend to the primary goals of the task at hand). Accordingly, CBT protocols offer a combination of informational, exposure, and cognitive restructuring interventions to bring about changes in the maladaptive thoughts, avoidance, and safety behaviors that derive from core fears of negative evaluation that help maintain social phobia. Meta-analytic review of the efficacy of these interventions indicates reliable improvement and maintenance of gains over time, with outcomes that rival those for pharmacologic treatment (see Fedoroff & Taylor, 2001; Gould et al., 1997).

COGNITIVE INTERVENTIONS

As patients learn to identify the role of thoughts in the social anxiety fear and avoidance cycle, the next steps are to help them coach themselves and intervene to (1) change their willingness to believe the negative thoughts that are currently active and (2) develop a more adaptive cognitive repertoire for guiding themselves.

Preparatory skills training for cognitive restructuring instructs patients to "stop and listen in on" the sort of things they are saying to themselves. In particular, you want your patients to do this whenever they experience increases in anxiety. However, it is not uncommon for patients to have initial difficulty completing cognitive tasks at moments of intense anxiety or during highly feared events. For many patients, it is difficult to evaluate thinking until after the anxiety has subsided or the situation has passed.

Hence, cognitive restructuring may involve moving the intervention "backward," starting with post-anxiety or post-situation evaluation of thoughts and working over time to notice these thoughts in real time. This process is aided by preparing patients for the form and content of anxiogenic thoughts. As in panic disorder, many of the negative and catastrophic thoughts will be a variant of "what if. . ." (e.g., "I hope it doesn't get worse," "What if it is like last time?" "What if other people notice?" "It will be just awful"). In other words, the prototypic social anxiety-related thoughts are future-oriented and tend to focus on the perceived consequences of social mishaps or the demonstration of anxiety symptoms to others. A list of Common Negative Thoughts in Social Anxiety Disorder is provided in the appendix and shown here as Table 9.1.

Cognitive interventions for social anxiety disorder follow the same principles as outlined in Chapters 3, 6, and 8. With Socratic questioning, patients are given the opportunity to identify their anxiogenic thoughts and evaluate their accuracy. An example follows.

> **C:** You mentioned that you get very anxious when you have to talk during social gatherings. When was the last time you experienced this?
>
> **P:** I went to a wedding last weekend and I was miserable the entire time.
>
> **C:** What was going through your mind when you were feeling miserable?
>
> **P:** I could swear that everyone there was looking at me.
>
> **C:** Who was getting married?
>
> **P:** A good friend from high school.
>
> **C:** So why do you think that everyone was looking at you on your friend's wedding day?
>
> **P:** I always feel that way when I have to talk during social gatherings.

Table 9.1 Common Negative Thoughts in Social Anxiety Disorder

- Fears of failure
  - I am not smart enough to answer the question correctly.
  - I am going to freeze up and be totally unable to get my idea across.
  - I am going to say the wrong thing and lose my job.
  - No one will want to be my friend if they see my anxiety.
- Fears of embarrassment and humiliation
  - I am going to drop the glass and everyone will turn around and look at me.
  - I am going to say the wrong thing, and he will think I'm an idiot.
  - I am going to start shaking and everyone will know I'm anxious.
  - Everyone will see I'm no good and something is wrong with me.

C: OK, what is it about talking during these social gatherings that makes you miserable?

P: Oh, I don't know. At the wedding I kept worrying that I would say something stupid.

C: Did that thought help?

P: No, the more I thought about how everything I might say was stupid, the more anxious I felt.

Comment:

Note that in this example, the clinician is able to probe for negative thoughts with the use of Socratic questioning. This largely consists of asking specific questions that allow the patient to elaborate on her experience in a specific social situation as well as the specific thoughts associated with negative appraisals of that experience (i.e., "What was going through your mind?"). The clinician then focuses on helping the patient identify the negative thoughts, as well as the relationship between such thoughts and symptoms of social anxiety (i.e., "Did that thought help?").

C: OK, let's review your experience at the wedding. You indicated that you felt miserable because you thought to yourself, "Everyone is looking at me." How often do you have this thought when you enter into a social situation?

P: All the time; it just pops in my head.

C: So during social situations you automatically think that everyone is focused on you?

P: Yeah, that's right.

C: Well, I want you to try the best you can to remember when you had that thought at the wedding and how you felt immediately afterwards.

P: I remember that I got really nervous and I eventually made up some excuse to leave the table.

C: So it seems like there might be a relationship between your negative automatic thoughts and your social anxiety.

P: What do you mean?

C: Well, based on what you report, when you have a negative automatic thought, your social anxiety increases, sometimes to the point where you have to escape and avoid the social situation.

P: Umm...

C: Tell me how many people were at the wedding.

P: Oh, I don't know, about 200.

C: That is quite a lot of people. How to do you know for certain that they were all looking at you and judging you?

P: I guess I don't know for certain—but I usually do feel like I'm the center of attention and everyone is staring at me.

C: So you cannot be 100% certain that people are staring at you and judging you, although it feels that way to you in social situations?

P: Well, I guess I can't be certain.

C: Do you suppose that at your friend's wedding most people would be looking at you?

P: Well, I guess they would probably be paying more attention to the bride.

Comment:

The clinician uses the example to help the patient learn that her commonly held fears may not be based on a correct estimation of the likelihood of others attending to her perceived flaws. Additional dialogue may also be useful to address overestimations of negative outcomes even if others do notice the patient's anxiety or if the patient does draw attention to herself.

C: So what happened when she introduced herself to you?

P: Oh, I totally freaked out—I mean, I got all hot, sweaty, and flushed—I could tell she noticed because she asked me if I was feeling OK.

C: What did you say?

P: Well, I was really feeling humiliated. I just kind of mumbled and said I was fine, just warm. I thought for sure I would pass out on the spot from embarrassment.

C: Did you?

P: No—actually I never have.

C: So it sounds like even when you do get anxious and others notice, although it feels very uncomfortable, your worst feared outcomes such as fainting from embarrassment may not occur. Does this seem correct to you?

STRUCTURING EXPOSURE

Situational exposure provides patients with opportunities to relearn or actually learn a sense of safety in avoided social situations. For promoting this therapeutic exposure, clinicians have three core strategies: (1) encouraging alternative strategies for use in the naturally occurring social exposures that patients endure, (2) structuring specific social exposures (e.g., public speaking) according to a hierarchy of graded items, or (3) structuring social mishap exposures to more directly target social-cost estimates for social errors. The first option provides the easiest approach in terms of session time but may be limited by the patient's avoidance patterns (i.e., few appropriate exposures may occur in a timely fashion) and over-learned avoidance (safety) behaviors in these situations. As such, options 2 and 3 are typically applied in CBT protocols.

However, prior to assigning these exposures as part of home practice, we recommend that clinicians first structure and complete an in-session exposure exercise. Although there is a clear time cost in a session for completing this exposure, it can be invaluable for informing the clinician about the degree and nature of a patient's self-critical and anxiogenic thoughts, and the rigidity of these beliefs as a social performance situation is confronted. In addition, it will help the patient gain necessary confidence to proceed with increasing exposures outside the office.

IN-OFFICE EXPOSURE INTERVENTION: PUBLIC SPEAKING

The goal of repeated exposures is to first help patients get comfortable with the feared sensations in the clinician's office, and to then practice these exposures at home. Given that fear of speaking is one of the most highly ranked and most commonly feared situations in social anxiety disorder, it is an excellent target for in-office exposures guided by the clinician. For example, the clinician may say:

> OK, now we have talked about some of the thoughts and excessive fears you have about embarrassing or humiliating yourself during presentations. One of the best ways to reduce your fear and avoidance of presentations is to get some practice with presentations right here in the office with me.

Although the ultimate goal of exposure work is to reduce anxiety in feared social and performance situations, it is important to clarify for the patient that this does NOT mean waiting until he or she is no longer anxious in the situation to approach it. On the contrary, we want the patient to go ahead and complete social exposures *even if anxious*, and to learn that he or she will be OK despite the presence of these symptoms. It is helpful to remind the patient prior to exposure exercises or the assignment of exposure as homework that anxiety associated with exposures is natural, and that the best way we know to reduce anxiety over time is to gain experience staying in feared situations, even if the patient feels anxious or frightened. Even though this can be difficult at times, this is how the patient will begin to reduce anxiety over time. Patients will notice that their anxiety is reduced as they master the exposure exercises and gain confidence staying in the situation until their initial anxiety decreases.

For a public speaking exposure, clinicians should follow these steps:

1. Provide rationale as just described.
2. Describe the plan to have the patient speak as much of 3 minutes as possible with the goal of discussing two points of interest during the 3-minute exercise.

3. Ask the patient to take a moment to select the two points he or she wants to cover before starting.

4. Instruct the patient to continue even if he or she starts to feel anxious. Remind patients before they start that the goal is to speak for as close to 3 minutes as possible and cover the two points, not to speak without anxiety.

5. Have the patient begin—if the patient hesitates, encourage him or her to continue if the two points haven't yet been covered (e.g., "You are doing great—please continue...")

6. After the speech is completed ask the patient how it went. Was it as expected? How anxious was the patient? Did his or her worst fears come true? (See discussion and sample dialogues of cognitive restructuring opportunity after the exposure below.) The most important point is to have the patient focus on the achievement of the goal—making a speech that includes two points—rather than avoiding anxiety, and to acknowledge that he or she accomplished this goal *despite* the presence of anxiety during the presentation.

It is important to note the degree to which the speaking exposure aids cognitive change. As patients have tolerable experiences with symptoms, they accrue greater evidence to dispute their catastrophic expectations. Accordingly, clinicians should take a moment to help this process along with questions like the following:

- *What do you make of this presentation exposure?*
- *Did your worst-case scenario occur?*
- *What thoughts are you having about it now?*

Also, clinicians should not hesitate to return to a cognitive restructuring approach for any increase in symptoms that may have occurred during the exposure, depending on the reaction to the exposure exercise.

C: Yes, I see you did experience an increase in anxiety with the presentation exercise. This is not surprising, as you are just learning how to feel comfortable with it. Can you tell me what thoughts you were having during the exposure?

P: I was thinking: I am really going to screw this up; I can't do this at all. I am a total idiot. Then I noticed I was getting anxious and had trouble expressing myself the way I wanted to and felt sure it was true.

C: Let's step back for a moment and check the facts. You said, "I can't do this at all." Did you do it?

P: Well... actually I guess I did—but I just knew it was lousy and I could have done so much better if I was not anxious.

C: Well, it might be true that you could find your words more easily if you were not anxious, but actually you did complete the speech anyway, and did get your point across to me despite your anxiety. Congratulations! What do you think?

P: Well, I still think it could have been much better. . . but I guess I did do it!

ASSIGNING OUT-OF-SESSION EXPOSURE

In designing situational exposure interventions for a patient, start at the social exposure level where he or she is currently. In other words, design an initial exposure that is only moderately harder than the patient's current level of functioning. The goal of initial exposure is to help the patient develop accurate expectations about what the process of successful exposure feels like, and to learn to meet goals in a situation despite having symptoms. After this initial exposure, the patient can then be assigned a more difficult exposure.

For whatever social exposures that are assigned, two instructions are especially important. First, during exposure practices patients should attend to what other people are doing. This attention is important for two reasons: it helps decrease self-focused attention, and it places attention on more relevant social stimuli (e.g., replacing "How am I doing?" or "I bet he notices I am sweating" with "What is he saying?" or "What is interesting about this conversation?"). It also allows patients to note whether negative outcomes are actually occurring (e.g., "I talked with a lot of people at the party," "She came up and started a conversation with me").

Second, patients should work to decrease safety behaviors. As noted in Chapter 4, safety behaviors are those things that patients do to try to avert catastrophic outcomes (e.g., "I averted my eyes so that I would not freeze up," "I stayed with my wife so she could bail me out if I froze up in a conversation," "I kept sipping water so that my voice would not quaver"). Use of these safety behaviors helps keep fears alive by preventing the learning of true safety (e.g., "I did OK even though I looked right at the listener's face").

Research has shown that these instructional conditions have important implications for fear reduction with exposure (Wells et al., 1995; Wells & Papageorgiou, 1998). In fact, research on these topics was motivated, in part, by the observation that many patients with social anxiety disorder will attempt social interactions (e.g., go to the cocktail party) but do not achieve anxiety reduction from these experiences (Wells et al., 1998). Hence, identifying and decreasing safety behaviors and helping patients to attend to what is happening outside of themselves in social situations may be crucial factors in changing ineffective social exposures into useful (and anxiety-reducing) learning experiences.

SOCIAL MISHAP EXPOSURE

Because core fears in social anxiety disorder include excessive concerns about embarrassment or humiliation due to minor imperfections in social and performance situations (including actual decreases in performance that may occur as a result of anxiety, or common day-to-day minor mistakes like spilling from a cup or forgetting a word), it is helpful to have the patient practice purposeful minor social mishaps and learn to be comfortable with them.

Social mishap exposures are used to help patients change their estimates of the social cost of minor social errors. These exposures are to be completed after patients have become adept at cognitive restructuring: that is, they are able to identify errors in thinking and social evaluation and are willing to examine actual outcomes and challenge preconceived notions that social errors are globally "horrible," "unacceptable," or "too embarrassing to bear." For these exposures patients are instructed to evaluate the actual negative consequences of the assigned social mishaps. In traditional CBT sessions, the clinician would accompany the patient on the initial social mishap exposure, helping the patient complete post-exposure evaluation of the outcome of the event. Subsequently, patients are to complete these exposures on their own, and report the results during the next session. Selection of the exposure is dependent on the patient's level of anxiety, with the goal of starting with an exposure that is deemed anxiety-provoking but tolerable. Examples of social mishap exposures follow, drawn from the list provided by Hofmann & Otto (2008, pp. 201–202):

- Ask multiple people (e.g., 10 people over a half an hour) in a specific and obvious location (e.g., immediately outside Fenway Park) where to find that location. Say, "Excuse me, I am looking for Fenway Park."
- Order coffee at a coffee bar and when it is handed to you, say: "Is this decaf?" Add without apologizing: "I would like to have mine decaf."
- Go to a video rental outlet and rent a DVD. Walk out and immediately back in requesting to return the DVD, saying: "I forgot I don't have a DVD player."
- Ask a bookstore clerk for the following two books: *The Kama Sutra* and *The Joy of Sex*. Ask the clerk which one he or she would recommend.
- Walk backward slowly on a crowded sidewalk for 3 minutes.

For these exposures, the social mishap task should be conceptualized as similar to a scene in a movie. The clinician is the movie director and the patient is the actor. The actor is to adhere to the script (and to observe objective outcomes), and to avoid safety behaviors such as over-apologizing (or apologizing at all, depending on the exposure).

THE PRESENCE OF ANXIETY SYMPTOMS

The presence of anxiety symptoms (e.g., a dry throat, flushed face, sweating) may act as a profound modulator of the patient's anxiety during exposure ("I am fine as long as I don't flush or tremble"). Accordingly, these symptoms may need to be intentionally included in exposure for successful reduction of social anxiety. Much like social mishap exposures, which ensure that patients decrease their fears of imperfect social performances, social exposures may need to include symptoms induced by interoceptive exposure. For example, patients may place their head below their knees to induce a red face prior to an assigned exposure. Patients are not to tell others the source of their symptoms, but to become adept at accepting their social performance regardless of the presence of the symptoms. In fuller CBT protocols, clinicians may use videotapes to provide objective feedback on social performance under these conditions.

SOCIAL ANXIETY DISORDER AND DEPRESSION

There is evidence that CBT can provide good outcomes for patients with social anxiety disorder despite the presence of comorbid depression (see Academic Moment, Box 9.2). Given these findings, we recommend vigorous treatment of social anxiety disorder with CBT even when depression is present, as long as both the clinician and patient judge the anxiety to be the primary disorder (and usual clinical safety assessments regarding potential suicidality have been made). In this treatment, additional efforts may need to be devoted to motivational issues, and cognitive restructuring may need to target depressive as well as anxiogenic cognitions. If the depression does not resolve with the resolution of social anxiety, additional sessions can be devoted exclusively to depression treatment. Treatment outcome studies support this sequential application of treatment targets (Woody, McLean, Taylor & Koch, 1999).

Box 9.2 Academic Moment: Comorbid Depression in Social Anxiety Disorder

Comorbidity between social anxiety disorder and depression is common and is generally associated with a greater severity of anxiety symptoms (e.g., Erwin, Heimberg, Juster & Mindlin, 2002), including even more negative evaluations of social performances (e.g., Ball et al., 1995). Comorbid depression may also affect the evaluation of success following exposure interventions (see Telch, 1988). However, despite this array of negative effects, CBT for social anxiety disorder (and, in fact, panic disorder) is often resistant to the negative effects of comorbid depression: as judged both by individual studies and meta-analytic review, patients with social anxiety disorder and depressive symptoms often improve to the same degree as those without these symptoms. For example, Erwin et al. (2002) found similar rates of improvement from CBT regardless of the presence of comorbid major depression, and in a meta-analytic review, Lincoln and Rief (2004) found that treatment outcome for social anxiety disorder did not differ depending on whether comorbid major depression was permitted or excluded from the clinical trial. Moreover, depression often improves with improvements in social anxiety: Moscovitch and colleagues (2005) found that social anxiety symptom improvement mediated 91% of subsequent depression symptom improvement.

SIGNS OF ADAPTIVE CHANGE

As already noted at the outset of this chapter, one common pattern of change in CBT for social anxiety disorder is a mid-treatment realization that social goals are met despite the presence of anxiety, followed by a subsequent decrease in anxiety as patients get more experience with their social success and realize that negative expectations about these situations are not realized. In other words, one important signpost of adaptive change appears to be the realization of a distinction between *feeling* anxious and *being* socially ineffective—that is, patients realize that anxiety is no longer a signal of actual social threat. In addition, some patients experience therapeutic gains upon realizing that their social anxiety is made up of peaking and ebbing distress ("I never persisted at the task long enough to realize my anxiety is strong for only half a minute"), and that the short-lived peaks are more tolerable than assumed. Patients also learn, particularly from social mishap exposures, that negative social outcomes do not portend the feared dire consequences. Repetition of exposure thereafter further decreases anxiety and enhances the sense of safety in social situations. With these improvements, anticipatory anxiety around social situations further decreases, helping eliminate the cascade of negative expectations and anxious affect that characterized the disorder. The clinician can then help the patient become oriented to seeking out more newly pleasurable social interactions and events.

10

CBT FOR INSOMNIA

CBT for insomnia is directed toward breaking the patterns that foster and maintain poor sleep by (1) educating patients about sleep-promoting habits, (2) addressing unhelpful beliefs about sleeping, and (3) helping patients to develop more regular and adaptive sleep patterns. To achieve these ends, CBT provides patients with training in stimulus control, sleep hygiene, cognitive interventions, sleep restriction, and relaxation techniques. Interventions like these have shown clear efficacy for insomnia, with meaningful improvements in 70% to 80% of patients and maintenance of treatment gains over time. Also, there are growing data supporting CBT-based interventions for sleep difficulties that co-occur with Axis I mood and anxiety disorders, with evidence that sleep interventions can speed recovery (see Academic Moment boxes throughout the chapter).

INFORMATIONAL INTERVENTIONS

- Provide instruction in sleep hygiene and stimulus-control procedures for sleep.
- Provide information on the role of thoughts in promoting insomnia.
- Monitor progress in follow-up visits.

CORE INTERVENTION ELEMENTS

- Provide an overview of sleep-interfering patterns.
- Provide instruction in sleep hygiene and stimulus control.
- Complete sleep-specific cognitive restructuring.
- Monitor current sleep patterns and determine optimal time in bed.

- Apply sleep prescription (sleep restriction) procedures.
- If needed, provide instruction in relaxation training.
- Monitor progress in follow-up visits.

STEPPED CARE: SLEEP HYGIENE

Minimal treatment for insomnia includes instruction in sleep hygiene. Sleep hygiene is a set of commonsense guidelines for sleep promotion. Although there is some overlap with the stimulus-control guidelines, sleep hygiene also focuses on daytime practices and environmental modifications that are conducive to good sleep. Much of the intervention can be covered by reviewing Table 10.1 with patients (also provided as a handout, Sleep Hygiene Guidelines, in the appendix), with follow-up review of adherence. In a stepped-care approach, this minimal intervention plus stimulus control is offered routinely to anyone with sleep difficulties (assuming adequate medical assessment has ruled out such disorders as sleep apnea and nocturnal myoclonus) as a first step. If difficulties continue, then a fuller set of cognitive-behavioral interventions can be considered. All interventions are relatively brief and the clinician can easily use a component approach for insomnia interventions. Also, given evidence that perceptions of sleep amount and quality are sometimes stronger determinants of disability than actual sleep levels (e.g., Semler & Harvey, 2005), some attention to cognitive distortions can be especially valuable for attenuating distress while fuller resolution of sleep difficulties is pending.

STIMULUS CONTROL

According to a cognitive-behavioral model of primary insomnia (e.g., Edinger & Means, 2005), cognitive factors such as misattributions about the causes of insomnia, unrealistic expectations about sleep needs, catastrophizing about the effects of sleep loss, and dysfunctional beliefs about sleep-promoting practices can interfere with sleep and motivate the use of strategies that further interfere with circadian rhythms (e.g., poor sleep scheduling), disrupt homeostatic regulation (e.g., spending excessive time in bed to recover lost sleep), and inhibit sleep onset and maintenance (e.g., poor sleep hygiene, conditioned anxious arousal to bed or sleep-related stimuli). Stimulus-control interventions are based on the notion that the stimuli associated with bedtime and the bedroom setting are associated with relaxation for normal sleepers, but in patients with insomnia, repeated unsuccessful sleep attempts have caused these same stimuli to be associated with increased arousal. Clinicians should explain to patients that the goal of stimulus-control therapy is to help re-associate the bed and bedroom with relaxation and successful sleep attempts. To this end, patients are given the set of

Table 10.1 Sleep Hygiene Guidelines

Guideline	Rationale
1. Limit the amount of time spent in bed and maintain a regular sleep/wake cycle.	Spending too much time in bed leads to shallower sleep and longer periods of wakefulness. Sticking to a regular bedtime and wake-up time will train your body's biological clock to be ready for sleep and ensures that you will be alert during the appropriate times of the day.
2. Get regular moderate exercise in the late afternoon or early evening.	Exercise will help to make you tired and it leads to deeper sleep at night. It is important not to exercise right before bed, since this can increase arousal and make it harder to fall asleep quickly.
3. Avoid exposure to bright lights at night.	This can interfere with your natural body clock by providing cues for wakefulness at night. Nightlights can also contribute to this problem.
4. Avoid heavy meals or drinking within 3 hours of bedtime.	Heavy meals and drinking liquids can increase the likelihood of heartburn, indigestion, and the need to urinate during the night.
5. Enhance your environment by making sure the bedroom is quiet, dark, and comfortable.	Temperatures below 75 degrees are most conducive to sleep. Ear plugs or a white-noise machine may help reduce noise. Blackout curtains may help keep the room dark. Remove work-related items from the bedroom.
6. Avoid caffeine, alcohol, and nicotine before bed.	Coffee, tea, chocolate, caffeinated soft drinks, and cigarettes contain stimulants that make it much harder to fall asleep. Drinking alcohol before bed may help with sleep onset but can lead to fragmented sleep.
7. Practice a relaxing bedtime routine.	This sends a signal to your body that it is time to wind down. It is important to stop all activating daytime activities at least 1.5 hours before bedtime.
8. Have a light bedtime snack.	This will help to manage awakenings due to hunger. Try including cheese, milk, or peanut butter. These types of snacks may help to make you drowsy.
9. Remove the bedroom clock.	Avoid "watching the clock" at night. This often serves as a reminder that you are not sleeping and leads to increased arousal and frustration.

Source: Edinger & Carney (2008); Kupfer & Reynolds (1997); NHLBI Working Group on Insomnia (1998).

Table 10.2 Sleep Stimulus-Control Guidelines

Guideline	Rationale
1. Go to bed only when sleepy.	Lie down in bed only when you are feeling tired and intend to go to sleep.
2. Use the bed or bedroom only for sleeping or sex.	When in bed it is important to avoid doing things that you would do when awake. Do not read, eat, watch TV, surf the Internet, talk on the phone, worry, or plan future events while in bed.
3. Get out of bed when unable to sleep.	If you are awake for more than 15 minutes, go to another room and return to the bedroom only when you feel like you really can fall asleep. Remember, the goal is to associate your bed with falling asleep quickly.
4. Get up at the same time every morning.	Do this regardless of how you slept the night before. Sleeping-in can disrupt your sleep schedule and keep you from becoming sleepy at the proper time the next night.
5. Avoid daytime napping.	Sleeping during the day partially satisfies your sleep needs and will weaken your natural sleep drive at night.

Source: Bootzin, Epstein & Wood (1991); Edinger & Carney (2008); Morin (2004).

guidelines in Table 10.2 (also provided as a handout, Sleep Stimulus-Control Guidelines, in the appendix) to add to their standard bedtime and wake-up time regimens.

Efforts should be made to ensure that patients understand the reasoning behind the stimulus-control guidelines to reduce problems with adherence to the stimulus-control interventions and time-in-bed prescriptions. It is important for patients to understand that treatment recommendations must be followed consistently to have a significant impact on long-term sleep habits.

Finally, clinicians should recognize *worry time* procedures (from Chapter 8) as another example of a stimulus-control procedure that can be used to help patients get control over chronic worry. These interventions may be helpful as part of broader stimulus-control and cognitive procedures (see below) for patients who complain that worry keeps them awake. For these patients, the interventions from Chapter 8, including worry time, may be the lead intervention, with sleep interventions used to add extra potency.

Box 10.1 Academic Moment: Efficacy of CBT for Sleep Problems

There is a great deal of evidence supporting the efficacy of cognitive-behavioral interventions for insomnia (Morin et al., 2006). For example, a large meta-analysis by Morin and colleagues (1994) of non-pharmacologic interventions for insomnia including data from 59 treatment outcome studies (2,102 participants) found that after completing an average of 5 hours of behavioral therapy, the average patient with sleep-onset problems was better off than 81% of untreated controls, and the average patient with sleep-maintenance problems was better off than 74% of untreated controls. Self-reported sleep latency decreased from approximately 60 minutes pre-treatment to 35 minutes post-treatment when averaging across behavioral techniques. Effect sizes were large for sleep latency ($d = 0.88$) and medium for time awake after sleep onset ($d = 0.65$). Morin and colleagues found stimulus control and sleep restriction therapy to be the most effective behavioral interventions, but other meta-analytic studies have reported no difference among various behavioral therapy techniques (Murtagh & Greenwood, 1995), although benefit over sleep hygiene instruction alone is clear (Edinger et al., 2009).

Behavioral treatments also perform well in comparison to pharmacotherapy for insomnia. In their meta-analytic review of 21 randomized trials (470 participants), Smith and colleagues (2002) examined acute treatment outcomes for patients treated with pharmacotherapy (flurazepam, lorazepam, temazepam, triazolam, quazepam, zolpidem) or behavioral therapy (stimulus control and/or sleep restriction). Wake time after sleep onset was reduced by 46% with pharmacotherapy and 56% with behavior therapy. Total sleep time improvements were modest in both treatments (12% for pharmacotherapy, 6% for CBT), and both treatments showed improvements in sleep quality (20% for pharmacotherapy, 28% for CBT). Results suggested that patients who were treated with CBT had significantly greater reductions in sleep latency than did those treated with pharmacotherapy (43% vs. 30%). Data from comparative treatment studies suggest that although both types of treatment may perform well initially, patients treated with CBT interventions show greater long-term maintenance of treatment gains (Morin, Colecchi, Stone, Sood & Brink, 1999).

The efficacy of combined psychopharmacological and cognitive-behavioral interventions for insomnia remains unclear (Mendelson, 2007). Some studies have shown no benefit of combined treatment over CBT alone for patients with sleep-onset insomnia (Jacobs et al., 2004), while others suggest a benefit to early combined treatment with medication discontinuation in the follow-up phase for patients with persistent insomnia (Morin et al., 2009; Vallières, Morin & Guay, 2005).

There are also some data to suggest that patients prefer behavioral over pharmacological interventions for insomnia (Morin et al., 1992; Vincent & Lionberg, 2001). Research further indicates that behavioral sleep interventions can be effectively delivered across a range of modalities. Bastien and colleagues (2004) compared CBT (including stimulus control, sleep restriction, cognitive interventions, and sleep hygiene) implemented in individual therapy, group therapy, or telephone consultation format. Results indicated that all three modalities led to significant improvements that were maintained at 6-month follow-up. Total wake time dropped in almost half, and participants showed 80% sleep efficiency following CBT interventions. Sleep efficiency ranged from 56% to 82% at follow-up. Recent studies suggest that brief cognitive-behavioral interventions (including stimulus control, sleep hygiene, sleep restriction, cognitive interventions, and/or relaxation training) presented in a self-help Internet format are also effective in improving sleep quality and reducing insomnia severity and daytime fatigue (Ritterband et al., 2009; Vincent & Lweycky, 2009).

COGNITIVE INTERVENTIONS

Patients with insomnia are likely to present with a number of maladaptive beliefs and attitudes about sleep that are involved in the development and maintenance of their sleep problems. Most individuals will experience transient or situational insomnia from time to time, but sleep problems are more likely to persist and become chronic if they are interpreted as a sign of danger or loss of control. As with panic disorder, it is not the symptom itself, but the patient's *interpretation* that amplifies the problem.

Cognitive interventions for insomnia provide an additional means of helping the patient change negative associations with the bedroom, the bed, and the process of getting to sleep. The goals of cognitive restructuring are (1) to eliminate anxiogenic, arousal-inducing, and catastrophic sleep-related thoughts during the night, (2) to help the patient engage in more realistic evaluations of his or her sleep performance and daytime functioning, and (3) to correct faulty beliefs about sleep-promoting practices and associated sleep-incompatible behaviors. It is also important to address patients' maladaptive beliefs regarding sleep as a preparation for sleep prescriptions, if used. For example, a patient who holds strongly to the belief that he needs 8 hours of sleep to function adequately will be unlikely to comply with a lesser time-in-bed prescription or to get out of bed if he does not fall asleep within 15 minutes.

Similar to the cognitive techniques used for other disorders, a preparatory step for cognitive restructuring in insomnia is to instruct patients to "stop and listen in on" the sort of things they are saying to themselves and how these may be related to their sleep problems. As patients learn to identify the role of thoughts in the development and maintenance of insomnia, the next steps are to help them intervene to (1) change their willingness to believe the negative thoughts that are currently active, (2) improve their ability to examine the evidence for or against these thoughts, and (3) develop a more realistic, helpful, and sleep-compatible cognitive repertoire. Patients may be asked to refer to information presented during sleep education and sleep hygiene interventions in order to challenge their maladaptive thoughts about sleep. Belanger and colleagues (2006) recommend that the clinician cue patients to these types of thoughts using some guided imagery, as illustrated by the following exchange between clinician and patient:

> **C:** Now I want you to close your eyes and imagine that it is 4 a.m. and you've been tossing and turning for hours. You have an important meeting tomorrow that you can't miss, but you can't seem to get to sleep. Tell me your thoughts at this moment.
>
> **P:** I'm thinking, "I'll never get to sleep. I've tried everything and nothing is working. . . I really have to impress my boss tomorrow because they've been cutting back. I don't know what will happen if I don't do well and get this client to sign a contract tomorrow. I've got to be alert in the morning. I'll probably get fired if I don't close this deal."

Once the patient has identified some of his maladaptive sleep-related cognitions, the clinician proceeds to use Socratic questioning to help the patient identify the consequences of thinking in this manner.

> **C:** And how are you feeling when you have these thoughts?
>
> **P:** I'm getting all wound up about it. Feeling tense, I guess, and much more anxious about how my meeting will go.
>
> **C:** I bet! Most of us would be feeling pretty upset if we thought the consequence of not falling asleep was being unable to function at work and getting fired. Sounds like you are telling yourself some pretty scary things about the consequences of your insomnia, and this actually makes you feel more anxious.
>
> **P:** It sure does.

If dysfunctional thoughts about sleeping are slow to change, clinicians can adopt the self-monitoring procedures from Chapter 3 to help patients further challenge their thoughts. However, cognitive interventions are only minimal components in many CBT programs for insomnia; in most cases, helping patients identify and change initial thoughts may be a sufficient cognitive intervention for insomnia. Table 10.3 lists common dysfunctional thoughts linked to sleep and is followed by a fuller example of cognitive restructuring for insomnia.

Table 10.3 Common Maladaptive Thoughts in Insomnia

- Unrealistic sleep expectations
  - I must get 8 hours of sleep every night.
  - The more sleep I get, the healthier I will be.
  - I should never wake up at night.
- Misattribution/exaggeration about the consequences of insomnia
  - My insomnia is a sign of serious health problems.
  - If I'm groggy in the morning I won't be able to get through the day.
- Incorrect beliefs about sleep-promoting practices
  - When I have trouble sleeping, I should stay in bed and try harder.
  - Naps are the only way to recover from a bad night of sleep.
- Catastrophizing
  - If I don't get to sleep right now, I am going to perform so badly I'm going to lose my job.
  - I'll go crazy from sleeplessness.

C: Ok, what percentage would you say that you believe the thought "I can't concentrate at all if I have a poor night of sleep"?

P: Umm... about 85%. I have a really hard time if I don't sleep well; I feel like my brain is mush.

C: Let's think of how we might test out this belief. Remind me again, how was your sleep last night?

P: Not too good. It took me a long time to fall asleep and I woke up a bunch of times.

C: Would you say this qualifies as a poor night of sleep?

P: Yup. It is pretty typical.

C: OK, so we could actually gather some evidence to see if your thought "I can't concentrate at all" is accurate. I've got a magazine here. Maybe we could have you read something to see if you are able to concentrate.

P: [*Takes magazine*] I guess I could try that.

C: Why don't you read the cover story about the hospital expansion?

P: [*Reads for a few minutes*] OK, I'm done.

C: What did you learn?

P: Well, they are planning to add a whole new wing to the children's hospital. The architects paid a lot of attention to making sure that all the patient rooms have windows so the kids can see out into this big garden. It actually sounds like a really nice place.

C: And what do you make of the fact that you were able to read the article and describe it to me? How does that fit with the belief that you can't concentrate at all?

P: OK, you got me. I guess I can focus long enough to read a short article like this. But there's no way I can concentrate on the technical projects I have to do at work. They are way too complicated.

C: So would it be more accurate to say that you sometimes have a hard time concentrating on certain tasks if you haven't slept well, but at other times you do OK?

P: I guess that is fair.

Comment:

This strategy of directly testing dysfunctional thoughts is also useful for helping patients to examine their incorrect beliefs regarding sleep-enhancing practices and to promote more adaptive sleep-related behaviors. For example, a patient who believed that daytime napping was essential to recover lost sleep would be asked to complete an experiment in which he or she refrained from naps for a specified number of days and observed the outcome on sleep quality and daytime functioning.

Box 10.2 Academic Moment: Sleep Problems in Patients with Affective Disorders

Research suggests that insomnia is a pervasive problem for patients with affective disorders and that these sleep problems may exacerbate or maintain co-occurring psychiatric symptoms. Among patients with depression, for example, insomnia is associated with greater severity of depression and increased suicidal ideation (Reynolds & Kupfer, 1984; Thase, 1999). Insomnia-type sleep disturbances have also been linked to poorer treatment response to antidepressant medications (Buysee et al., 1997; Dew et al., 1997; Winokur & Reynolds, 1994) and appear to be a significant risk factor for relapse (Brower et al., 2001; Reynolds et al., 1997). Moreover, there is emerging evidence that cognitive-behavioral or pharmacologic treatment of sleep difficulties aids the treatment of depression (Fava et al., 2006; Morawetz, 2003; Taylor et al, 2007) and generalized anxiety disorder (Pollack et al., 2008), supporting the notion that these interventions targeting sleep may have additional effects on the treatment of the primary affective disorder.

Cognitive-behavioral interventions for sleep have been shown to offer greater long-term efficacy than pharmacologic interventions in both comparative treatment studies and meta-analytic reviews (e.g., Jacobs, Pace-Schott, Stickgold & Otto, 2004; Morin, Colecchi, Stone, Sood & Brink, 1999; Morin, Culbert & Schwartz, 1994; Morin et al., 2006), making the addition of this treatment to ongoing treatment of affective disorders an especially appealing intervention. In addition, there is encouragement from the literature that sleep interventions can offer some benefit for PTSD either with a primary or secondary focus on nightmare amelioration (Davis & Wright, 2007; Germain, Shear, Hall & Buysse, 2007) or without this focus (Smith, Huang & Manber, 2005).

SLEEP MONITORING

Sleep monitoring provides valuable information regarding the nature of the patient's sleep problems and forms the basis of the patient's time-in-bed prescription (see section that follows), if that intervention is needed. Daily sleep monitoring should be introduced early in treatment, since it is also used to guide the selection and implementation of later strategies. The Sleep Diary provides patients with a place to record time to bed, how long it took to fall asleep, waking time, out-of-bed time, use of naps, and ratings of sleep quality and feeling rested. Additional relevant information includes the frequency of nighttime awakenings, use of prescription or nonprescription sleep aids (e.g., alcohol), and/or timing of stimulant (e.g., caffeine, nicotine) use. For time in bed prescriptions, two weeks of sleep monitoring is commonly used, particularly for the calculation of average sleep time. A Weekly Sleep Diary is shown here and additional copies for patient use are provided in the appendix.

Box 10.3 Weekly Sleep Diary

Weekly Sleep Diary: (Week of × 10)

Date/ Day	Time to Bed	Time to Fall Asleep	Waking Time	Hours Slept	Nap Taken	Sleep Meds	Sleep Qual. (0–3)	Feel Rested (0–3)
					Y N	Y N		
					Y N	Y N		
					Y N	Y N		
					Y N	Y N		
					Y N	Y N		
					Y N	Y N		
					Y N	Y N		

Note: Sleep Quality and Feeling Rested are rated on a 0 (low/bad) to 3 (excellent) scale.

Comments:

_____

_____

SLEEP RESTRICTION: TIME-IN-BED PRESCRIPTIONS

Once the patient has completed the sleep diaries, the clinician can calculate his or her average sleep time and provide a recommendation for the actual amount of time the patient should spend in bed each night. Average sleep time is calculated by summing

139 CBT for Insomnia

the number of minutes slept each day and dividing this by the number of days the patient recorded in his or her sleep diary. The time in bed prescription is calculated by taking the average sleep time and adding 30 minutes (to allow sufficient time to fall asleep and for a few brief awakenings). For patients who are getting very little sleep, the time-in-bed prescription should not be set for less than 5 hours per night. The goal is to increase sleep efficiency by consolidating the sleep level the patient is currently achieving. The clinician and patient then work together to choose a standard daily bedtime and wake-up time so that the time-in-bed prescription can be followed. This prescription may significantly shift time in bed—time that is spent in maladaptive patterns of waiting for sleep. The goal of sleep restriction is to decrease the time allotted for sleep each night such that the time spent in bed closely matches the patient's actual sleep needs. This is accomplished by adjusting the time-in-bed prescription depending on the patient's sleep performance and daytime functioning after the patient has followed the original sleep schedule for approximately 2 weeks.

Changes to the time-in-bed prescription are made based on the patient's average sleep efficiency, which is calculated by taking the ratio of time spent asleep to time spent in bed. For example, a patient who slept for 7.5 hours after spending 10 hours in bed would have a sleep efficiency of 75% (7.5/10 = 0.75). If the patient has not reached 85% sleep efficiency with the original time-in-bed prescription, adjustments are made to reach this target. For those who report sleep efficiency of greater than 90% but are still feeling tired during the day, the clinician may add 15 to 20 minutes to the time-in-bed prescription. This adjustment is made until the patient reports that he or she regularly sleeps through the night and feels rested in the morning. For patients reporting sleep efficiency of less than 85%, the time-in-bed prescription may be reduced by 15 to 20 minutes until the patient is able to sleep soundly without excessive periods of wakefulness. Some patients may require additional reductions in order to increase their natural sleep drive. The rationale for sleep restriction is presented in more detail in the following section.

It is important for the patient to take an active role in setting up the sleep schedule and in making needed adjustments, as this is likely to improve adherence to treatment recommendations. It is also important for patients to understand that, although they may feel more fatigued initially due to a reduction in the time they are spending in bed, most patients will see improvements in their insomnia within a couple of weeks of beginning treatment; many patients have a return to normal sleep patterns within 8 weeks of implementing treatment recommendations. However, treatment will be successful only if patients consistently apply the agreed-upon behavioral and cognitive strategies.

Because restrictions in time in bed (to improve sleep efficiency) will seem paradoxical to some patients, it is important for the clinician to allow sufficient time to fully explain the rationale for sleep restriction prior to implementing this intervention.

C: I can tell from your sleep diary that you've done a great job keeping to the sleep schedule over the past week, but it's still taking you quite some time to fall asleep. Is that right?

P: Yeah, I get in bed at the time we agreed on last session, but I'm just not tired enough to fall asleep.

C: I think we have another tool that should help with this. This is going to sound counterintuitive, but what you have told me actually means that we have to adjust your sleep prescription. We gave you too much time in bed!

P: You want me to cut back on my sleeping time even more? I don't get it. I just finished saying that I haven't been able to fall asleep. . .

C: Believe it or not, we've found that *reducing* the amount of time you spend in bed will actually *increase* your body's natural sleep drive and make it more likely that you can fall asleep at bedtime!

P: Really? You've lost me on this one. . .

C: Restricting your sleep time will help to reduce the amount of time you spend lying awake in your bed worrying about how hard it is to fall asleep, and it will also give your body the chance to get tired again. So in the short term we actually *want* you to feel sleepier during the day, since this will make your body increasingly ready and able to fall sleep when bedtime arrives.

P: That is what I've been trying to avoid. Maybe I had the wrong idea, but I thought it was bad to be tired during the day. . .

C: This actually may not be a bad thing at all. We can capitalize on your daytime fatigue to help get you back to a more regular sleep pattern. With sleep restriction it is normal and desirable for you to feel more tired during the day. In the first week or so of your new sleep regimen, you will probably notice an increase in daytime sleepiness. This may be uncomfortable, but it is not harmful to you. That said, during this period it is best not to engage in activities that would be dangerous to do when you are very tired. These are things like driving long distances or operating heavy machinery. Most other daily activities are fine.

Comment:

It is also helpful to refer to evidence from the patient's sleep diaries to guide this discussion. For example, point out those nights that the patient went to sleep later in the evening (i.e., stayed awake for more hours of the day) and spent less time falling asleep after he or she got in bed.

C: Maybe it would help to take a look at your sleep diary. I see here that you went to bed at 11 p.m. on Tuesday and it took about 45 minutes for you to fall asleep. It looks like you were awake for about 16 hours that day. But here, on Friday, you went to bed at 12:30 and it only took 20 minutes for you to fall asleep. Looks like you were awake for 18 hours on that day.

P: Oh, I didn't notice that. So if I stay up later I might actually be able to fall asleep quicker. That is opposite of what I thought it would be.

C: Right, but the trick is to limit your total sleep time, so if we set your bedtime to be a couple of hours later, you still need to get up at the same time each morning. Let's have you try this new schedule for a couple of weeks. If you are able to stick with it for a week or so and are still feeling tired during the day, we can increase your time in bed. Just like we would do with a medication, we'll continue to monitor and adjust your sleep prescription until we get to the right dose for you.

As illustrated in this example, the patient's wake-up time is typically kept the same but bedtime is delayed. If the patient is used to getting into bed much earlier than the new bedtime, it is important to discuss with the patient what he or she will do to stay awake until bedtime. This may involve engaging in physical activity (e.g., taking a walk), participating in an engaging activity (e.g., playing chess, doing a crossword), or socializing with others. Activities such as reading or watching television are to be avoided, since these may increase the likelihood of the patient falling asleep before the established bedtime.

RELAXATION TRAINING

Relaxation techniques may be a helpful sleep intervention, particularly for patients who report physical or emotional tension that interferes with sleep. In such cases, relaxation training is often used as a method of reducing bedtime arousal and sleep-related performance anxiety. Various relaxation techniques can be used to help the patient physically and emotionally prepare for bedtime. These include progressive muscle relaxation, cued relaxation, biofeedback, imagery training, diaphragmatic breathing, and/or meditation practices. Selection of techniques is generally based on patient preference. Information on progressive muscle relaxation training is offered in Chapter 5.

USE OF MEDICATIONS WITH CBT

Benzodiazepines and non-benzodiazepine hypnotics have been widely used to treat insomnia due to their acute effects on sleep. Use of these medications while undergoing CBT for insomnia is not necessarily contraindicated, although medication does not appear to confer additional benefits over CBT alone. These medications also carry a risk of tolerance, reduced efficacy, and abuse over time. Patients may express interest in reducing or discontinuing their use of hypnotic agents while participating in CBT. Medication discontinuation does not appear to have any negative effects on CBT, but patients should be cautioned that stopping these medications abruptly can lead to rebound insomnia. Cognitive-behavioral interventions have also been successfully used to help with benzodiazepine discontinuation. Patients who undergo tapered withdrawal from hypnotics while participating in CBT may see additional improvements in sleep quality. If you have applied CBT while the patient is on medication, a booster session after medication taper may be helpful to extend and maintain treatment gains.

Box 10.4 Academic Moment: CBT and Pharmacotherapy for Insomnia

There is evidence for the efficacy of CBT for facilitating discontinuation of benzodiazepines among chronic hypnotic users. For example, Morin and colleagues (2004) compared the efficacy of a supervised 10-week slow taper, group CBT, and CBT combined with a slow taper for benzodiazepine discontinuation in a sample of 76 older adults with chronic insomnia and prolonged benzodiazepine use (mean = 19.3 years). Results indicated improvements in sleep and significant reductions in benzodiazepine use for all three groups, but there was a greater likelihood of being medication-free for participants in the combined treatment condition (85%) compared to slow taper alone (48%) or CBT alone (54%). Participants who received CBT also reported greater improvements in total sleep time relative to those who received the medication taper alone. No significant withdrawal symptoms were reported. Other studies have also reported reductions in use of hypnotic medications even among patients enrolled in CBT interventions that did not directly target medication discontinuation (Morgan, Dixon, Mathers, Thompson & Tomeny, 2004). Discontinuation of hypnotics during CBT does not appear to have any negative impact on treatment efficacy and may confer additional improvements in sleep efficiency and wake after sleep onset (Zavesicka, Brunovsky, Matousek & Sos, 2008).

11

CASE CONSULTATIONS: CBT AND PHARMACOTHERAPY

Combination treatment (psychotherapy and pharmacotherapy) is common in clinical practice. This chapter focuses on some of the questions that arise as part of combination therapy. Using a question-and-answer format, responses to case scenarios offer guidance for issues that may arise for clinicians who will be providing CBT to patients who are currently taking or are considering taking medications.

STARTING TREATMENT FOR SOCIAL ANXIETY DISORDER

Bob, a 43-year-old single man, comes to treatment with a history of marked social anxiety since childhood, with difficulties dating and socializing and problems speaking up during meetings at work. He has generally avoided performance situations such as public speaking and his anxiety in most social situations has interfered with his ability to seek a promotion at work; he has remained at an entry-level position for years despite having the skills to advance. Though hoping to marry and raise a family, his anxiety has made it difficult to initiate and maintain romantic relationships. He has never before sought treatment for his social anxiety but comes in after seeing a magazine advertisement for medication for social phobia, and he reports a family member who responded positively to an SSRI for anxiety and depression.

What is the role of CBT for this individual, given that I am confident that the patient will achieve at least some benefit from SSRI treatment?

The available evidence suggests that this patient can benefit from pharmacotherapy, CBT, or their combination, and there is no reliable empirical evidence to help the clinician decide which treatment will be optimal. Regardless of which approach is selected initially, it is important to provide the patient with a sense of the range of treatments that may provide benefit and help him understand that if the initial treatment does not provide adequate benefit, others will be tried. Providing the patient with the sense that there are multiple therapeutic tools for change may help keep the patient in treatment if there is a poor response to initial interventions. In addition, if pharmacologic care is to be selected as the initial intervention, it is important to initiate treatment in a way that will support later psychosocial interventions if needed. Patients should be informed that they could improve from either CBT or pharmacotherapy, and avoid exclusively biological models for care (e.g., "You will need medications to improve," "For you to get better, we need to correct an imbalance in neurotransmitters"), which may have the unfortunate effect of dampening acceptance for CBT if it is required later on in the course of treatment. Instead, it is preferable to suggest that there are multiple successful ways to tackle anxiety, with medication being one approach thought to target neurotransmitters as a means of change, and psychotherapy being another, directly targeting cognitions and behaviors; evidence supports that both approaches can result in remission of anxiety disorders.

WORRY, ANXIETY, AND IRRITABILITY

Helen is a 26-year-old married woman working as a manager for a large financial services company. She has experienced marked anxiety since adolescence, with excessive worries about her relationships, health, and finances despite stability in each of these areas. Associated symptoms include sleep disturbance (initial insomnia), irritable bowel, muscle tension, and frequent irritability. She presented for treatment about 6 weeks ago after her husband suggested that her anxiety and irritability were getting worse and starting to negatively affect their relationship. She was started on paroxetine 20 mg, increased to 40 mg after a month, and though she has noted some improvement, she remains markedly anxious with persistent worries, difficulties relaxing, sleep disturbance, and irritability.

What should I attend to in providing CBT interventions for this patient?

Cognitive restructuring interventions (Chapter 3) represent an excellent option for the worry-based patterns exhibited by Helen. Time needs to be devoted to helping her understand the role of worry in maintaining anxiety patterns, and the importance of learning to react differently to these worries, including the restructuring of worries and adoption of a more adaptive problem-solving approach (Chapter 5) for life stressors. Also, given evidence of her chronic arousal, irritability, and somatic and sleep symptoms, relaxation interventions have an important role in helping Helen start to develop new affective patterns. While significant benefit may be achieved with relaxation training alone, given her level of chronic distress, it might be better to start with an integrated strategy of managing her schedule (discussing breaks, pleasant events, and the worry time intervention), educating her about the nature of anxiogenic thoughts, and introducing relaxation training at the same time. Receiving a multicomponent intervention at the outset may best meet her expectations for her different symptoms. Coordination of these components will take a longer session than a traditional medication visit but may pay off in terms of better adherence to interventions should she experience immediate benefits. If this multicomponent, longer-session approach is not feasible, each component can be rolled out over a series of shorter visits.

NONRESPONSE TO SSRIs PLUS BENZODIAZEPINES

Nancy is a 34-year-old married mother of two with an 8-year history of recurrent panic attacks and phobic anxiety of crowded places such as supermarkets, and frank avoidance of driving outside her immediate neighborhood. At the time of initial treatment 3 years ago, Nancy had been essentially homebound, afraid to venture far from her house because of fear of recurrent attacks that were occurring three or four times per week, and her husband had assumed most of the responsibilities for shopping and transporting their two small children to school and other activities. She initiated treatment with the SSRI sertraline titrated up to 200 mg/day, with the benzodiazepine clonazepam 3 mg/day later added after there was little response to the SSRI alone. Her symptoms had improved to the point that she was able to leave the house and drive in her immediate neighborhood, but her attempts to increase her activities were associated with a marked increase in her panic attacks, and she often took an "as-needed" dose of the clonazepam whenever she was about to enter a store or drive, or when she felt the beginnings of a panic attack. She was frequently worried about having panic attacks, especially if she were alone somewhere with her children, concerned she would be overwhelmed and unable to care for them.

Should I think about CBT for this patient; after all, she appears very treatment-resistant?

Despite the striking limited response to pharmacotherapy for this patient, available studies suggest that clinicians can still be confident of improvements with short-term CBT for medication-resistant panic disorder. With such strong agoraphobia and fears of anxiety symptoms, interoceptive exposure is a very important component of CBT that will provide the patient with a model of how to react differently to symptoms. The treating clinician can start this process by trying to understand the patient's core fears

("What tells you that you will be overwhelmed if you feel anxious?" "What do you think would happen if you just stayed in the situation and let yourself be anxious?" "What would lead you to be unable to care for your children?"). Initial answers to these questions should be followed by further Socratic questioning, as exemplified in Chapters 3 and 6. Chapter 6 also describes the initiation of step-by-step exposure, starting at a level where the patient is willing to complete exposures without taking a PRN dose of clonazepam. Unfortunately, PRN use of benzodiazepines is common and can directly interfere with the patient's ability to learn that she can tolerate exposure to feared situations and sensations; this is one reason it is best to stabilize dosing of concurrent benzodiazepines to standing daily doses at set times, if at all possible, prior to initiating CBT interventions. The goal is to help the patient see that she can succeed in her tasks, despite the initial presence of anxiety and without the use of a PRN dose. Treatment progress would likely be aided substantially by in-session completion of interoceptive exposure, but even without these interventions, the patient should learn increased comfort in the presence of anxiety sensations as part of her success in persisting in once-avoided situations.

ANXIOUS, WORRIED, AND NOW DEPRESSED AGAIN

Joe is a 57-year-old accountant with a long history of generalized anxiety and recurrent major depression, with a recent exacerbation of his anxiety and mood symptoms following the end of his marriage of 30 years. He has been experiencing an increase in general feelings of tension and ruminative worry, decrease in self-esteem, sleep disturbance including initial insomnia and mid-awakening, headaches, poor concentration, anhedonia, lack of motivation to participate in anything but essential activities, and marked irritability. His work performance has deteriorated and his boss has commented on it—he is making uncharacteristic errors and is brusque and unpleasant with co-workers and clients. He reports that he started a benzodiazepine but it made him feel dulled, and that an SSRI subsequently initiated made him feel too jittery, so he discontinued both. He reports feeling hopeless that any treatment intervention will be helpful.

I have the sense that this patient needs an antidepressant to achieve improvement in his depression and anxiety, but given his sensitivity to side effects, is CBT an option?

Prior medication nonresponse does not preclude response to CBT, and the presence of depression comorbid with anxiety does not demand the use of antidepressants in treatment. Indeed, there is evidence that anxiety will often improve with CBT at the same rate in individuals with and without depression, and that the depression itself often improves following CBT for anxiety disorders (for review see Deveney & Otto, 2010). Nonetheless, depressed patients are likely to be more severe at the start of treatment, and may need more attention to challenging negative thoughts and maintaining motivation. More closely spaced sessions (including standard safety monitoring) and more emphasis on re-establishing pleasant events and activities as part of exposure assignments may aid cognitive restructuring efforts. We placed our chapter on GAD after the chapters on panic and depression to illustrate that the combination of approaches for anxiety and depression is frequently helpful for GAD. For this individual, pleasant event assignments and the use of worry time interventions, rather than reliance on an overly cognitive treatment, may be especially important.

ADDRESSING ALCOHOL ABUSE

Chris is a 20-year-old college student who has been generally shy and socially anxious since childhood. While in high school he discovered that he felt more comfortable at parties and other social situations if he had a few drinks prior to attending. Since starting college, with the increase in social interactions both in and outside the classroom, Chris has started having "a few drinks" most days before leaving his room to attend class or go to a social event, and on at least two occasions in the past 6 months he has drunk to the point of blacking out at a party. He was referred by the student counseling service after his grades began to fall and he was in danger of being placed on academic probation. While he realizes that he has "lost control" of his alcohol use, he notes that the alcohol helps him feel more comfortable and function better in class and in social situations.

I have the sense with this patient that he might respond well to interventions for social anxiety if his alcohol use does not get in the way. Any suggestions?

Motivational interviewing interventions are designed to help the patient realize and utilize his own motivations for seeking alternatives to alcohol use. With this patient, it will be important to identify one of the core motivations for alcohol use: to get control over the social anxiety. Starting with this perceived beneficial use, the clinician can start helping the patient identify both the positive and negative aspects of alcohol use, and then examine whether other strategies for his goals are available. A nice "signpost" for success in the process is the patient noting, "I need to find a better way of controlling my anxiety; this alcohol use is just getting me in trouble." With this opening, the clinician can then discuss the "tools" available for this goal, including CBT (Chapter 9) or pharmacologic interventions.

EXPOSURE ASSIGNMENTS BRING FEAR AND ESCAPE

Kathy is a 40-year-old woman with a history of panic disorder with significant phobic avoid-ance since her mid-20s. She has been on an SSRI for years, which has eliminated her panic attacks, and she has minimal daily anticipatory anxiety, which may be largely attributable to her continued avoidance of phobic triggers such as exercise, heights, and crowds. Attempts to structure a gradual exposure hierarchy for the patient have been unsuccessful as she reports that as soon as she enters a feared situation she becomes overwhelmed with anxiety and flees.

How can I better help this patient with the exposure I think she needs?

When patients feel overwhelmed by anxiety during initial exposure attempts, the cli-nician has a range of options for success. One should always think how the exposure exercise can be divided into smaller and more manageable units. The goal is to help the patient develop a "map for success" before moving on to more anxiety-provoking items. Although it is tempting to focus only on making the situation less challenging (e.g., exposure to smaller stores, closer to home), this intervention misses the essential point that the cue for fleeing appears to be the experience with anxiety. Hence, the experience of anxiety needs to be central to the practice of new patterns. For example, an important starting point in this process is active rehearsal of responding differently to minor levels of anxiety using interoceptive exposure. The goal is to help the patient become more comfortable with symptoms in order to eliminate her desire to flee. During this process, urges to flee and the reasons for these urges should be actively discussed. Review of cognitive interventions in the context of interoceptive exposure— "What is it like feeling these sensations and doing nothing (not fleeing)?" "What do you think might happen if you stayed in the [feared] situation even though you had these sensations?"—is an important part of this process. As the patient becomes more comfortable experiencing higher and higher levels of anxiety sensations, she is ready to begin rehearsing having these sensations in feared situations. For this process, the relevant home practice assignment is to complete interoceptive exposure in feared situations (this ensures that sensations occur and helps eliminate the maladaptive habit of desperately trying not to get anxious in these situations); the goal is to practice being comfortable with anxiety sensations (and inducing these sensations) in the feared situation. For patients with partially controlled panic dis-order on medications, it is also helpful to understand what they believe the implica-tions of anxiety sensations while on medications may be, including fears of losing this partial symptom reduction (in this case, freedom from panic attacks) they have attributed to the medication.

BUT I NEED THE PILLS; I CAN'T STAND TO
BE WITHOUT THEM

Susan is a 28-year-old recently married lawyer with a history of panic disorder that has been well controlled over the past 3 years on 20 mg/day escitalopram and 2.5 mg/day clonazepam. She and her husband are hoping to start a family in the next year and she wishes to try to discontinue her medication. However, even with a slow taper of the benzodiazepine, she experiences a return of her anticipatory anxiety and episodic panic attacks, as well as persistent feelings of jitteriness, lightheadedness, and stomach distress, which she attributes to withdrawal. She wonders if she is becoming a "hypochondriac," noting an increasing focus on relatively minor somatic symptoms, and fears a return of her full-blown panic disorder.

What should my focus be if I start CBT?

Even with control of anxiety symptoms while on medication, fears of symptoms may remain and be triggered by the anxiety-like symptoms that re-emerge upon medication taper (as a result of benzodiazepine withdrawal or the re-emergence of the disorder). Regardless of cause, the return of symptoms upon benzodiazepine discontinuation tends to be the rule rather than the exception. Similar concerns may also be present around attempts at antidepressant discontinuation, particularly for patients who closely monitor somatic sensations such as dizziness that may occur with SSRI discontinuation. Research suggests that cognitive and exposure-based interventions directed at the fear of symptoms can greatly improve the likelihood that patients can discontinue medication treatment. Interoceptive exposure, with the goal of helping the patient react differently to symptoms regardless of whether they are disorder-based or the result of a return of anxiety patterns or medication discontinuation, is perhaps the most important component intervention. This training in responding differently to symptoms should start before the taper, and taper-related symptoms should be treated as another form of interoceptive exposure—the patient is to do nothing to try to control these symptoms. Fuller protocols are available for benzodiazepine discontinuation in patients with panic disorder (Otto & Pollack, 2009).

Appendix of Forms and Handouts

Thought Record
List of Cognitive Errors
Weekly Activity Schedule
Pleasant Events List
Planned Activity List
Steps to Goal Attainment
Problem-Solving Worksheet
Exposure Planning Checklist
Cognitive-Behavioral Model of Panic Disorder
Common Anxiogenic Thoughts in Panic Disorder
Common Negative Thoughts in Depression
Common Fears in Generalized Anxiety Disorder
CBT Model of Social Anxiety Disorder
Common Negative Thoughts in Social Anxiety Disorder
Sleep Hygiene Guidelines
Sleep Stimulus-Control Guidelines
Weekly Sleep Diaries
Exercise Planning Worksheet
Exercise for Mood Log

THOUGHT RECORD

Situation (Describe the event that led to the unpleasant emotion)	Emotion (Specify sad, angry, etc., and rate the emotion from 0% to 100%)	Automatic thought (Write the automatic thought and rate your belief in the thought from 0% to 100%)	Evaluation of automatic thought (Evaluate the accuracy of the automatic thought)	Re-rate emotion (Re-rate the emotion and your belief in the thought from 0% to 100%)

LIST OF COGNITIVE ERRORS

All-or-Nothing Thinking: Thinking in black-and-white terms; there are no gray areas. This type of thinking is unrealistic because things are seldom all or nothing, good or bad.

Overgeneralization: Assuming that a one-time negative occurrence will happen again and again; using words like "always" or "never" to make generalizations.

Mental Filter: Focusing exclusively on negative details and ignoring anything positive. Filtering out the positives causes you to see the entire situation as negative.

Disqualifying the Positive: Turning positives into negatives by insisting they "don't count." This allows you to maintain a negative outlook despite positive experiences.

Jumping to Conclusions: Jumping to negative conclusions in the absence of solid evidence. There are two types of this thinking: "mind reading" and the "fortune teller error." *Mind Reading* is assuming that you know what someone else is thinking. You are so convinced that the person is having a negative reaction to you, you don't even take the time to confirm your guess. In the *Fortune Teller Error*, you act like a fortune-teller who predicts only the worst for you. You then treat your unrealistic prediction as if it were a proven fact.

Magnification (Catastrophizing) or Minimization: Magnifying negative things means blowing their importance out of proportion; the outcome of an event appears catastrophic to you.

Minimizing positive things means shrinking their significance; you make good experiences out to be smaller than they are.

Emotional Reasoning: You take your emotions as proof of the way things really are. You assume something is true because you feel it is.

"Should" Statements:You build your expectations with "shoulds," "musts," and "oughts." When you don't follow through, you feel guilty. When others disappoint you, you feel angry and resentful.

Labeling and Mislabeling: You label yourself or someone else, rather than just identifying the behavior. You mislabel an event by using inaccurate and emotionally extreme language.

Personalization: You take responsibility for things that you don't have control over. You feel guilty because you assume a negative event is your fault.

Adapted from Burns (1980)

WEEKLY ACTIVITY SCHEDULE

	Morning	Midday	Afternoon	Evening
Monday				
Tuesday				
Wednesday				
Thursday				
Friday				
Saturday				
Sunday				

PLEASANT EVENTS LIST

The following list is designed to stimulate ideas for activities that may increase your weekly pleasure level as well as provide stress-buffering effects. In considering this list, think of the *variations on themes* that may make an activity especially rewarding. For example, little things added to a regular activity—buying your favorite childhood candy at the movie theater or fixing a cup of tea to drink while reading a novel—can help transform an experience by evoking past pleasant memories.

As you go through the list, check off those activities of most interest to you.

☐ Go fishing in a local stream or pond	☐ Read the newspaper in a coffee shop
☐ Call two friends and go bowling	☐ Schedule a kissing-only date with your romantic partner
☐ Play with a Frisbee	☐ Order hot chocolate in a restaurant
☐ Take a kid to mini golf	☐ Buy flowers for the house
☐ Take a yoga class	☐ Get a massage
☐ Go to an indoor rock-climbing center—take a lesson	☐ Reread a book you read in high school or college
☐ Build a snow fort and have a snowball fight	☐ Bake cookies for a neighbor
☐ Walk in the snow and listen to your footsteps	☐ Have a garage sale (perhaps with a neighbor)
☐ Catch snowflakes in your mouth	☐ Buy a spool of wire and make a sculpture
☐ Sign up for a sculpting class	☐ Go to an art museum and find one piece you really like
☐ Bake a cake	☐ Buy a magazine on a topic you know nothing about
☐ Draw	☐ Polish all of your shoes
☐ Paint (oils, acrylics, watercolor)	☐ Buy a new plant
☐ Climb a tree	☐ Clean out a closet
☐ Go for an evening drive	☐ Write a letter to the editor of the local newspaper
☐ Go to a drive-in movie	☐ Repaint a table or a shelf
☐ See a movie	☐ Go to a diner for breakfast
☐ Volunteer to work at a soup kitchen	☐ Devote a meal to cooking red, white, and blue foods
☐ Join a museum Friday night event	☐ Plan an affordable 3-day vacation
☐ Write a letter to a friend	☐ Start a collection of heart-shaped rocks
☐ Sing a song	☐ Find your top three favorite videos on YouTube and share them with a friend

☐ Play a musical instrument	☐ Woodworking—build a table or a chair
☐ Take an art class	☐ Burn a CD of your favorite movie music
☐ Walk a dog	☐ Take a dance class
☐ Volunteer to walk dogs for a local animal shelter	☐ Learn to fold dollar bills into origami creatures
☐ Play with children	☐ Soak your feet in warm water
☐ Visit a pet shop and look at the animals	☐ Learn to juggle
☐ Sit in the sun	☐ Clean and polish the inside of your car
☐ Sit on a porch swing	☐ Go to a concert
☐ Go for a hike	☐ Meditate
☐ Learn to knit	☐ Organize a weekly game of cribbage or bridge
☐ Do a crossword puzzle (each day for a week)	☐ Look at a map
☐ Go out for an ice cream sundae	☐ Plan a drive in the country
☐ Rent a garden plot at a local farm or community space	☐ Sew some napkins
☐ Grill dinner in the back yard	☐ Make a pizza and bake it
☐ Take a bath at night with candles around the tub	☐ Buy a cookbook and make three new meals
☐ Have a picnic at a park with a friend	☐ Read a novel
☐ Have a tea party on your or your neighbor's front porch	☐ Listen to your favorite song from high school... really loudly
☐ Go bird/nature watching	☐ Rent a video, make popcorn, and invite friends over
☐ Read a book under a tree	☐ Attend a local art event (a dance performance, a play, an art show opening)
☐ Organize photos/CD collection	☐ Go to a comedy club
☐ Write poetry	☐ Join a book club
☐ Join a choir or singing group	☐ Join an after-school program to mentor children
☐ Do Sudoku puzzles	☐ Lie by a pool/river/lake/beach
☐ Put on some dance music and dance in your living room	☐ Take a historic tour of your city
☐ Sign up for a class at the local community college or center	☐ Get dressed up and go out for dinner with your romantic partner or friends
☐ Make a scrapbook	☐ Have a neighborhood barbeque

☐ Read travel books about places you've always wanted to visit (and maybe plan a visit!)	☐ Take a photo every day for a week
☐ Play charades	☐ Have a poker night
☐ Go to the beach	☐ Go to a sporting event
☐ Go to the zoo	☐ Play ping-pong
☐ Start writing a journal	☐ Invite friends over for board games
☐ Learn a new language	☐ Play video games

PLANNED ACTIVITY LIST

For the planned activity list, consider items for both *pleasure* and a *sense of achievement*. The goal is to plan a return to activities that are naturally rewarding and that can act as an antidepressant. In your list, select items of varying degrees of difficulty (challenge), and remember that, because of your depression, feelings of motivation may be low. For these assignments, it may be necessary to "do them first," and then "feel like doing them" only after you have completed a number of the rewarding activities.

PLANNED ACTIVITY LIST

Item	Activity	Level of Difficulty
1		
2		
3		
4		
5		
6		
7		
8		
9		
10		
11		
12		

STEPS TO GOAL ATTAINMENT

Long-Term Goal Sheet
Long-term goal:

_____

_____

_____

	Short-term goal:
	Skill needed to achieve this goal:
	Short-term goal:
	Skill needed to achieve this goal:
	Short-term goal:
	Skill needed to achieve this goal:
	Short-term goal:
	Skill needed o achieve this goal:
	Short-term goal:
	Skill needed to achieve this goal:

NOW Your current situation: _____

_____

_____

PROBLEM-SOLVING WORKSHEET

What is the problem?
Why does this problem bother me (what are the specific features that bother me)?
Is this a realistic problem (e.g., what do I really think is going to happen, and what part of this problem do I think is just worry)?
How can I rewrite the problem clearly so that it helps me think about a solution? Write a clear restatement of the problem.
Now that I have the problem clearly in mind, what are potential solutions to this problem? To generate solutions, I want to think about as many solutions as possible (without thinking why they are good or bad, and without choosing an option at this point). What advice might a good friend give? If a friend had this problem, what advice would I give? Potential options:
Now rate each potential option. For each option rate the good and bad aspects of the proposed solution. Do not select an option until each is rated.   Good things about each solution Bad things about each solution   1.   2.   3.   4.   5.   6.   Given this evaluation, which solution seems best?
Do you want to apply this solution, or is more time or more information needed to solve this problem?

EXPOSURE PLANNING CHECKLIST

Attending to the Correct Core Fear:

What is/are the core fear or fears that should be targeted by treatment? Ask the patient: "What is so bad about…" to elucidate the central feared features.

_____

_____

_____

Attending to the Contexts Surrounding the Fear:

Aggravating Contexts

What are the contexts in which this fear is worse? Consider the following:

- Time of day/year (including light/dark, certain weather conditions, such as hot weather in the case of panic disorder): _____
- Presence of others (known or unknown people): _____
- Presence of symptoms (e.g., muscle tension, certain worries): _____
- Mental or physical fatigue (also including menstrual cycle): _____
- Interpersonal conflict: _____
- Other: _____
- Other: _____

Safety Behaviors/Events

What are the behaviors or events that lead the patient to assume relative safety from the feared outcomes?

- Contact with others (e.g., cell phone, presence of safe other, knowledge of availability of safe other): _____
- Food or drink (bottle of water, mints, antacids, crackers, fruit): _____
- Something to hold (glass)/position near a wall or door: _____
- Medication (often a benzodiazepine or beta-blocker): _____
- Cognitive rituals (e.g., affirmations, lucky sayings): _____
- Body positions/eye contact (averting one's eyes while speaking, clasping the hands, leaning against a wall, bracing against a chair): _____
- Talking with others: _____
- Other: _____
- Other: _____
- Other: _____

COGNITIVE-BEHAVIORAL MODEL OF PANIC DISORDER

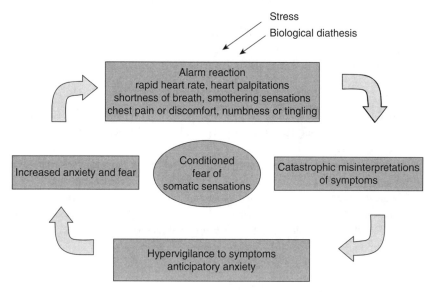

Reprinted from Powers, M. B., Vervliet, B., Smits, J. A. J., & Otto, M. W. (2010). Helping exposure succeed: Learning theory perspectives on treatment resistance and relapse. In M. W. Otto & S. G. Hofmann (Eds.), *Avoiding treatment failures in the anxiety disorders* (pp. 31–49). New York: Springer. With kind permission of Springer Science+Business Media.

COMMON ANXIOGENIC THOUGHTS IN PANIC DISORDER

In the anxiety disorders, two distortions in thinking are especially common:

(1) Overestimation of the probability of negative outcomes (e.g., "I will faint;" "I will have a heart attack;" "I will have to run out of the room"), and

(2) Overestimation of the degree of catastrophe of these outcomes ("It will be horrible;" "I will never recover").

Negative thoughts also feel dire because they are in the form of a prediction of a feared future event ("what if…") and global negative terms (e.g., "unbearable, horrible, terrible") are used to describe feared outcomes.

You and your clinician will be working to help you develop more accurate thinking patterns as part of interventions to eliminate the cycle of negative expectations and interpretations of anxiety and its symptoms. To help you in this process, it will be important for you to get to know some of the negative thoughts that are common in panic disorder. Take a look at the list below, and see which thoughts are closest to those that are part of your panic pattern.

- Fears of death or disability
  - Am I having a heart attack?
  - I am having a stroke!
  - I am going to suffocate!
- Fears of losing control/insanity
  - I am going to lose control and scream.
  - I am having a nervous breakdown.
  - If I don't escape, I will go crazy.
- Fears of humiliation or embarrassment
  - People will think something is wrong with me.
  - They will think I am a lunatic.
  - I will faint and be embarrassed.

Your goal will be to sap the power of these thoughts and to develop more useful patterns of thinking. Strategies for challenging such negative thoughts include asking yourself the following questions as part of developing a more accurate way of coaching yourself around frightening panic-related thoughts:

- What is the worst that could happen? Would I live through it?
- What's the best that could happen?
- What's the most realistic outcome?
- What is the effect of my believing the automatic thought?
- If a friend were in this situation and had this thought, what would I tell him/her?

COMMON NEGATIVE THOUGHTS IN DEPRESSION

When people get depressed, both their memories and their expectations of future events get more negative. That is, your mood can influence your beliefs about the past, present, and future, making it feel like things did not work out for you in the past, and that things won't work out for you in the future. In treatment, you will be working with your clinician to remember that your thoughts are simply mood-based guesses about the world rather than statements of reality. As part of treatment, it will be helpful for you to be ready for the negative thoughts that come to mind, and to be prepared to challenge these thoughts. Common negative thoughts in depression include:

- Negative thoughts about the self
  - I am a loser.
  - I am not lovable.
  - I am a failure.
- Negative thoughts about the future
  - I will never be happy.
  - Nothing will work out for me.
  - I will always be alone.
- Negative thoughts about the world
  - I will be rejected.
  - The deck is stacked against me.
  - Nothing good ever happens.

Strategies for challenging such negative thoughts include asking yourself the following questions as part of developing a more accurate way of coaching yourself around the negative thoughts that occur in depression:

- What is the worst that could happen? Would I live through it?
- What's the best that could happen?
- What's the most realistic outcome?
- What is the effect of my believing the automatic thought?
- If a friend were in this situation and had this thought, what would I tell him/her?

COMMON FEARS IN GENERALIZED ANXIETY DISORDER

In the anxiety disorders, two distortions in thinking are especially common:

(1) Overestimation of the probability of negative outcomes (e.g., "I will get sick;" "I will get fired;" "The kids will get hurt"), and

(2) Overestimation of the degree of catastrophe of these outcomes ("It will be horrible;" "I can't cope," "I would lose everything").

Negative thoughts also feel dire because they are in the form of a prediction of a feared future event ("what if…") and global negative terms (e.g., "unbearable, horrible, terrible") are used to describe feared outcomes.

You and your clinician will be working to help you develop more accurate thinking patterns as part of interventions to eliminate patterns of chronic worry. To help you with this process, it will be important for you to get to know some of the negative thoughts that are common in generalized anxiety disorder. Take a look at the list below, and see which thoughts are closest to those that are part of your worry pattern.

- Fears of unpredictable or uncontrollable events
  - I couldn't handle it if I got sick.
  - If I don't worry about this, I'll be caught off guard by something horrible.
- Fears of failure
  - I am going to mess up on this project and lose my job.
  - If I don't get an A on the test, I'm going to fail this class.
- Fears of uncertainty
  - I can't handle not knowing how it will go.
  - I have to check just to make sure everything is OK.

In treatment, your goal will be to sap the power of these thoughts and to develop more useful patterns of thinking. Strategies for challenging such negative thoughts include asking yourself the following questions as part of developing a more accurate way of coaching yourself around frightening thoughts that make up your worry pattern:

- What is the worst that could happen? Would I live through it?
- What's the best that could happen?
- What's the most realistic outcome?
- What is the effect of my believing the automatic thought?
- If a friend were in this situation and had this thought, what would I tell him/her?

CBT MODEL OF SOCIAL ANXIETY DISORDER

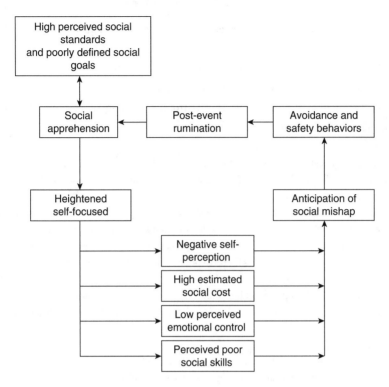

(Reprinted from Hofmann, S. G. (2007). Cognitive factors that maintain social anxiety disorder: A comprehensive model and its treatment implications. Cognitive Behavior Therapy, Vol 36:4, pp. 195–209, Taylor & Francis Ltd.)

COMMON NEGATIVE THOUGHTS IN SOCIAL ANXIETY DISORDER

In the anxiety disorders, two distortions in thinking are especially common:

(1) Overestimation of the probability of negative outcomes (e.g., "I will faint;" "I will have a heart attack;" "I will have to run out of the room"), and
(2) Overestimation of the degree of catastrophe of these outcomes ("It will be horrible;" "I will never recover").

Negative thoughts also feel more dire because they are in the form of a prediction of a feared future event ("what if…") and global negative terms (e.g., "unbearable, horrible, terrible") are used to describe feared outcomes.

You and your clinician will be working to help you develop more accurate thinking patterns as part of interventions to eliminate the cycle of negative expectations and interpretations of how you are doing socially. To help you in this process, it will be important for you to get to know some of the negative thoughts that are common in social anxiety disorder. Many of these thoughts have to do with negative predictions about how you will perform socially or negative predictions ("mind reading") about how others will view your performance. Take a look at the list below, and see which thoughts are closest to those that are part of your anxiety pattern.

- Fears of failure
  - I am not smart enough to answer the question correctly.
  - I am going to freeze up and be totally unable to get my idea across.
  - I am going to say the wrong thing, and lose my job.
  - No one will want to be my friend if they see my anxiety.
- Fears of embarrassment and humiliation
  - I am going to drop the glass and everyone will turn around and look at me.
  - I am going to say the wrong thing, and he will think I'm an idiot.
  - I am going to start shaking and everyone will know I'm anxious.
  - Everyone will see I am no good and something is wrong with me.

In treatment, your goal will be to sap the power of these thoughts and to develop more useful patterns of thinking. Strategies for challenging such negative thoughts include asking yourself the following questions as part of developing a more accurate way of coaching yourself around frightening thoughts that make up your worry pattern:

- What is the worst that could happen? Would I live through it?
- What's the best that could happen?
- What's the most realistic outcome?
- What is the effect of my believing the automatic thought?
- If a friend were in this situation and had this thought, what would I tell him/her?

SLEEP HYGIENE GUIDELINES

Guideline	Rationale
Limit the amount of time spent in bed and maintain a regular sleep/wake cycle.	Spending too much time in bed leads to shallower sleep and longer periods of wakefulness. Sticking to a regular bedtime and wake-up time will train your body's biological clock to be ready for sleep and ensures that you will be alert during the appropriate times of the day.
Get regular moderate exercise in the late afternoon or early evening.	Exercise will help make you tired and leads to deeper sleep at night. It is important not to exercise right before bed, since this can increase arousal and make it harder to fall asleep quickly.
Avoid exposure to bright lights at night.	This can interfere with your natural body clock by providing cues for wakefulness at night. Nightlights can also contribute to this problem.
Avoid heavy meals or drinking within 3 hours of bedtime.	Heavy meals and drinking liquids can increase the likelihood of heartburn, indigestion, and the need to urinate during the night.
Enhance your environment by making sure the bedroom is quiet, dark, and comfortable.	Temperatures below 75 degrees are most conducive to sleep. Ear plugs or a white-noise machine may help reduce noise. Blackout curtains may help keep the room dark. Remove work-related items from the bedroom.
Avoid caffeine, alcohol, and nicotine before bed.	Coffee, tea, chocolate, caffeinated soft drinks, and cigarettes contain stimulants that make it much harder to fall asleep. Drinking alcohol before bed may help with sleep onset but can lead to fragmented sleep.
Practice a relaxing bedtime routine.	This sends a signal to your body that it is time to wind down. It is important to stop all activating daytime activities at least 1.5 hours before bedtime.
Have a light bedtime snack.	This will help to manage awakenings due to hunger. Try including cheese, milk, or peanut butter. These types of snacks may help to make you drowsy.
Remove the bedroom clock.	Avoid "watching the clock" at night. This often serves as a reminder that you are not sleeping and leads to increased arousal and frustration.

Source: Edinger & Carney (2008); Kupfer & Reynolds (1997); NHLBI Working Group on Insomnia (1998)

SLEEP STIMULUS-CONTROL GUIDELINES

Guideline	Rationale
Go to bed only when sleepy.	Lie down in bed only when you are feeling tired and intend to go to sleep.
Use the bed or bedroom only for sleeping or sex.	When in bed it is important to avoid doing things that you would do when awake. Do not read, eat, watch TV, surf the Internet, talk on the phone, worry, or plan future events while in bed.
Get out of bed when unable to sleep.	If you are awake for more than 15 minutes, go to another room and return to the bedroom only when you feel like you really can fall asleep. Remember, the goal is to associate your bed with falling asleep quickly.
Get up at the same time every morning.	Do this regardless of how you slept the night before. Sleeping-in can disrupt your sleep schedule and keep you from becoming sleepy at the proper time the next night.
Avoid daytime napping.	Sleeping during the day partially satisfies your sleep needs and will weaken your natural sleep drive at night.
Source: Bootzin, Epstein & Wood (1991); Edinger & Carney (2008); Morin (2004).	

WEEKLY SLEEP DIARIES

Weekly Sleep Diary: (Week of)								
Date/ Day	Time to Bed	Time to Fall Asleep	Waking Time	Hours Slept	Nap Taken	Sleep Meds	Sleep Qual. (0–3)	Feel Rested (0–3)
					Y N	Y N		
					Y N	Y N		
					Y N	Y N		
					Y N	Y N		
					Y N	Y N		
					Y N	Y N		
					Y N	Y N		

Note: Sleep Quality and Feeling Rested are rated on a 0 (low/bad) to 3 (excellent) scale.

Comments:

Weekly Sleep Diary: (Week of)								
Date/ Day	Time to Bed	Time to Fall Asleep	Waking Time	Hours Slept	Nap Taken	Sleep Meds	Sleep Qual. (0-3)	Feel Rested (0-3)
					Y N	Y N		
					Y N	Y N		
					Y N	Y N		
					Y N	Y N		
					Y N	Y N		
					Y N	Y N		
					Y N	Y N		

Note: Sleep Quality and Feeling Rested are rated on a 0 (low/bad) to 3 (excellent) scale.

Comments:

EXERCISE PLANNING WORKSHEET

As part of the treatment of your mood or anxiety disorder, your clinician has chosen to recommend exercise. Research shows that exercise can be a powerful force in helping people recover from depression and anxiety. Before starting an exercise program for your mood, it is important that you and your clinician assess your overall state of physical health, and that you start with an exercise regimen that is within your current fitness limits. By starting slowly, and giving yourself a program of slowly increasing exertion over time, you can find an exercise program that will serve you well over time.

Also, starting a new program of regular exercise can be challenging. Everyday life events can interfere with your exercise plans, but the good news is that many of the obstacles are both predictable and avoidable. The exercise planning worksheet is used to help you think through some of the exercise and schedule challenges you may face, and what you can do about these challenges, so you can create and maintain a regular exercise program for your mood.

My exercise schedule for this week is as follows:			
Monday Activity: _____ Intensity: _____ Duration: _____	Tuesday Activity: _____ Intensity: _____ Duration: _____	Wednesday Activity: _____ Intensity: _____ Duration: _____	Thursday Activity: _____ Intensity: _____ Duration: _____
Friday Activity: _____ Intensity: _____ Duration: _____	Saturday Activity: _____ Intensity: _____ Duration: _____	Sunday Activity: _____ Intensity: _____ Duration: _____	SUMMARY Intensity: _____ Duration: _____ Frequency: _____

Anticipated barriers	*Possible solutions*
1.	1.
	2.
	3.
2.	1.
	2.
	3.

Adapted from Otto & Smits (2009)

EXERCISE FOR MOOD LOG

This log is to help me keep track of my exercise goals for mood by focusing on the importance of exercise several days a week.

Week Number _____

	Day 1 Date: ___/___	Day 2 Date: ___/___	Day 3 Date: ___/___	Day 4 Date: ___/___	Day 5 Date: ___/___	Day 6 Date: ___/___	Day 7 Date: ___/___
Day of the week							
Exercise completed (✓)							
Time of day of exercise							
Type of exercise completed							
Intensity (%HRmax)							
Duration (minutes)							
Pre-exercise Feelings/ Mood							
Post-exercise Feelings/ Mood							

Reprinted from Otto & Smits (2009)

REFERENCES

Abramson, L. Y., Seligman, M. E. P., & Teasdale, J. D. (1978). Learned helplessness in humans: Critique and reformulation. *Journal of Abnormal Psychology, 87*, 49–74.

American College of Sports Medicine. (2005). *ACSM's guidelines for exercise testing and prescription (6th ed.)*. Philadelphia, PA: Lippincott Williams, & Wilkins.

American Psychiatric Association. (2000). *Diagnostic and statistical manual of mental disorders* (4th ed. text revision). Washington, DC: Author.

Amir, N., Foa, E. B., & Coles, M. E. (1998). Automatic activation and strategic avoidance of threat-relevant information in social phobia. *Journal of Abnormal Psychology, 107*, 285–290.

Ball, S. G., Otto, M. W., Pollack, M. H., Uccello, R., & Rosenbaum, J. F. (1995). Differentiating social phobia and panic disorder: A test of core beliefs. *Cognitive Research and Therapy, 19*, 473–482.

Barlow, D. H. (2004). *Anxiety and its disorders: The nature and treatment of anxiety and panic* (2nd ed.). New York: Guilford Press.

Barlow, D. H., & Craske, M. G. (2006). *Mastery of your anxiety and panic: Workbook.* New York: Oxford University Press.

Barlow, D. H., Gorman, J. M., Shear, M.K., & Woods, S. W. (2000). Cognitive-behavioral therapy, imipramine, or their combination for panic disorder: A randomized controlled trial. *Journal of the American Medical Association, 283*, 2529–2536.

Basoglu, M., Lax, T., Kasvikis, Y., & Marks, I. M. (1988). Predictors of improvement in obsessive-compulsive disorder. *Journal of Anxiety Disorders, 2*(4), 299–317.

Basoglu, M., Marks, I. M., Kilic, C., Brewin, C. R., & Swinson, R. P. (1994). Alprazolam and exposure for panic disorder with agoraphobia: Attribution of improvement to medication predicts subsequent relapse. *British Journal of Psychiatry, 164*, 652–659.

Bastien, C. H., Morin, C. M., Ouellet, M. C., Blais, F. C., & Bouchard, S. (2004). Cognitive-behavioral therapy for insomnia: Comparison of individual therapy, group therapy, and telephone consultations. *Journal of Consulting and Clinical Psychology, 72*, 653–659.

Beck, A. T. (1967). *Depression: Causes and treatment.* Philadelphia: University of Pennsylvania Press.

Beck, A. T., Rush, A. J., Shaw, B. F., & Emery, G. (1979). *Cognitive therapy of depression.* New York: Guilford Press.

Beck, J. S. (1995). *Cognitive therapy: Basics and beyond.* New York: Guilford Press.

Behar, E., DiMarco, I. D., Hekler, E. B., Mohlman, J., & Staples, A. M. (2009). Current theoretical models of generalized anxiety disorder (GAD): Conceptual review and treatment implications. *Journal of Anxiety Disorders, 23*, 1011–1023.

Belanger, L., Savard, J., & Morin, C. M. (2006). Clinical management of insomnia using cognitive therapy. *Behavioral Sleep Medicine, 4*, 179–198.

Bell, A. C., & D'Zurilla, T. J. (2009). Problem-solving therapy for depression: A meta-analysis. *Clinical Psychology Review, 29*, 348–353.

Bernstein, D. A., & Borkovec, T. D. (1973). *Progressive relaxation training: A manual for the helping professions.* Champaign, IL: Research Press.

Biondi, M., & Picardi, A. (2003). Increased probability of remaining in remission from panic disorder with agoraphobia after drug treatment in patients who received concurrent cognitive-behavioural therapy: A follow-up study. *Psychotherapy and Psychosomatics, 72*(1), 34–42.

Blumenthal, J. A., Babyak, M. A., Moore, K. A., Craighead, W. E., Herman, S., Khatri, et al. (1999). Effects of exercise training on older patients with major depression. *Archives of Internal Medicine, 159,* 2349–2356.

Bonner, B. L. & Everett, F. L. (1982). Influence of client preparation and therapist prognostic expectations on children's attitudes and expectations of psychotherapy. *Journal of Clinical Child Psychology, 11,* 202–208.

Bootzin, R. R., Epstein, D., & Wood, J. M. (1991). Stimulus control instructions. In P. J. Hauri (Ed.), *Case studies in insomnia* (pp. 19–28). New York: Plenum.

Borkovec, T. D., Alcaine, O., & Behar, E. (2004). Avoidance theory of worry and generalized anxiety disorder. In R. G. Heimberg, C. L. Turk, & D. S. Mennin (Eds.), *Generalized anxiety disorder: Advances in research and practice* (pp. 77–108). New York: Guilford Press.

Borkovec, T. D., Wilkinson, L., Folensbee, R., & Lerman, C. (1983). Stimulus control applications to the treatment of worry. *Behaviour Research and Therapy, 21,* 247–251.

Bouton, M. E., Mineka, S., & Barlow, D. H. (2001). A modern learning-theory perspective on the etiology of panic disorder. *Psychological Review, 108,* 4–32.

Bradley, B. P., Mogg, K., & Lee. S. C. (1997). Attentional biases for negative information in induced and naturally occurring dysphoria. *Behaviour Research and Therapy, 35,* 911–927

Broocks, A., Bandelow, B., Pekrun, G., George, A., Meyer, T., Bartman, U., et al. (1998). Comparison of aerobic exercise, clomipramine, and placebo in the treatment of panic disorder. *American Journal of Psychiatry, 155,* 603–609.

Brower, K. J., Aldrich, M. S., Robinson, E. A., Zucker, R. A., & Greden, J. F. (2001). Insomnia, self-medication, and relapse to alcoholism. *American Journal of Psychiatry, 158,* 399–404.

Brown, R. A., Kahler, C. W., Zvolensky, M. J., Lejuez, C. W., & Ramsey, S. E. (2001). Anxiety sensitivity: relationship to negative affect smoking and smoking cessation in smokers with past major depressive disorder. *Addictive Behaviors, 26,* 887–899.

Brown, T. A., O'Leary, T. A., & Barlow, D. H. (2001). Generalized anxiety disorder. In D. H. Barlow (Ed.), *Clinical handbook of psychological disorders: A step-by-step treatment manual* (3rd ed., pp. 154–208). New York: Guilford Press.

Burns, D. D. (1980). *Feeling Good: The new mood therapy (Revised and Updated).* New York: Avon Books.

Carr, R. E., Lehrer, P. M., & Hochron, S. M. (1995). Predictors of panic-fear in asthma. *Health Psychology, 14,* 421–426.

Chambless, D. L., & Gracely, E. J. (1989). Fear of fear and the anxiety disorders. *Cognitive Therapy and Research, 13*(1), 9–20.

Clark, D. M., & McManus, F. (2002). Information processing in social phobia. *Biological Psychiatry, 51,* 92–100.

Davis, J. L., & Wright, D. C. (2007). Randomized clinical trial for treatment of chronic nightmares in trauma-exposed adults. *Journal of Traumatic Stress, 20,* 123–133.

Day, L., & Reznikoff, M. (1980). Preparation of children and parents for treatment at a children's psychiatric clinic through videotaped modeling. *Journal of Consulting and Clinical Psychology, 48,* 303–304.

Del Vecchio, T., & O'Leary, K. D. (2004). Effectiveness of anger treatments for specific anger problems: A meta-analytic review. *Clinical Psychology Review, 24,* 15–34.

Deveney, C. M., & Otto, M. W. (2010). Resolving treatment complications associated with comorbid depression. In M. W. Otto & S. G. Hofmann (Eds.), *Avoiding treatment failures in the anxiety disorders* (pp. 231–249). New York: Springer.

Dew, M. A., Reynolds, C. F., III, Houck, P. R., Hall, M., Buysse, D. J., Frank, E., et al. (1997). Temporal profiles of the course of depression during treatment. Predictors of pathways toward recovery in the elderly. *Archives of General Psychiatry, 54,* 1016–1024.

Dimidjian, S., Hollon, S. D., Dobson, K. S., Schmaling, K. B., Kohlenberg, R. J., Addis, M. E., et al. (2006). Randomized trial of behavioral activation, cognitive therapy, and antidepressant medication in the acute treatment of adults with major depression. *Journal of Consulting and Clinical Psychology, 74,* 658–670.

Dobson, K. S., Hollon, S. D., Dimidjian, S., Schmaling, K. B., Kohlenberg, R. J., Gallop, R. J., et al. (2008). Randomized trial of behavioral activation, cognitive therapy, and antidepressant medication in the prevention of relapse and recurrence in major depression. *Journal of Consulting and Clinical Psychology, 76,* 468–477.

Dugas, M. J., Gagnon, F., Ladouceur, R., & Freeston, M. H. (1998). Generalized anxiety disorder: A preliminary test of a conceptual model. *Behaviour Research and Therapy, 36,* 215–226.

Dugas, M. J., & Robichaud, M. (2006). *Cognitive-behavioral treatment for generalized anxiety disorder: From science to practice.* New York: Routledge.

Edinger, J. D., & Carney, C. E. (2008). *Overcoming insomnia: A cognitive behavioral therapy approach.* New York: Oxford University Press.

Edinger, J. D., & Means, M. K. (2005). Cognitive-behavioral therapy for primary insomnia. *Clinical Psychology Review, 25,* 539–558.

Edinger, J. D., Olsen, M. K., Stechuchak, K. M., Means, M. K., Lineberger, M. D., Kirby, A., & Carney, C. E. (2009). Cognitive behavioral therapy for patients with primary insomnia or insomnia associated predominantly with mixed psychiatric disorders: a randomized clinical trial. *Sleep, 32,* 499–510.

Ehlers, A. (1995). A 1-year prospective study of panic attacks: Clinical course and factors associated with maintenance. *Journal of Abnormal Psychology, 104,* 164–172.

Ehlers, A., Mayou, R. A., & Bryant, B. (1998). Psychological predictors of chronic posttraumatic stress disorder after motor vehicle accidents. *Journal of Abnormal Psychology, 107*(3), 508–519.

Erwin, B. A., Heimberg, R. G., Juster, H. R., & Mindlin, M. (2002). Comorbid anxiety and mood disorders among persons with social anxiety disorder. *Behaviour Research and Therapy, 40,* 19–35.

Fava, M., McCall, W. V., Krystal, A., Wessel, T., Rubens, R., Caron, J., et al. (2006). Eszopiclone co-administered with fluoxetine in patients with insomnia coexisting with major depressive disorder. *Biological Psychiatry, 59,* 1052–1060.

Fedoroff, I. C., & Taylor, S. (2001). Psychological and pharmacological treatments of social phobia: A meta-analysis. *Journal of Clinical Psychopharmacology, 21,* 311–324.

Ferster, C. B. (1973). A functional analysis of depression. *American Psychologist, 28,* 857–870.

Foa, E. B., & Kozak, M. J. (1986). Emotional processing of fear: Exposure to corrective information. *Psychological Bulletin, 99,* 20–35.

Gardenswartz, C. A., & Craske, M. E. (2001). Prevention of panic disorder. *Behavior Therapy, 32,* 725–737.

Germain, A., Shear, M. K., Hall, M., & Buysse, D. J. (2007). Effects of a brief behavioral treatment for PTSD-related sleep disturbances: A pilot study. *Behaviour Research and Therapy, 45*, 627–632.

Gilboa-Schechtman, E., Erhard-Weiss, D., & Jeczemien, P. (2002). Interpersonal deficits meet cognitive biases: Memory for facial expressions in depressed and anxious men and women. *Psychiatry Research, 113*, 279–293.

Gortner, E. T., Gollan, J. K., Dobson, K. S., & Jacobson, N. S. (1998). Cognitive–behavioral treatment for depression: Relapse prevention. *Journal of Consulting and Clinical Psychology, 66*, 377–384.

Gotlib, I. H., Krasnoperova, E., Neubauer, Y., Yue, D., & Joorman, J. (2004). Attentional biases for negative interpersonal stimuli in clinical depression. *Journal of Abnormal Psychology, 113*, 127–135.

Gould, R. A., Buckminster, S., Pollack, M. H., Otto, M. W., & Yap, L. (1997). Cognitive-behavioral and pharmacological treatment for social phobia: A meta-analysis. *Clinical Psychology: Science and Practice, 4*, 291–306.

Gould, R. A., Otto, M. W., & Pollack, M. H. (1995). A meta-analysis of treatment outcome for panic disorder. *Clinical Psychology Review, 15*, 819–844.

Gould, R. A., Safren, S. A., Washington, D. O., & Otto, M.W. (2004). A meta-analytic review of cognitive-behavioral treatments. In R.G. Heimberg, C. A. Turk, & D. S. Mennin (Eds.), *Generalized anxiety disorder: Advances in research and practice* (pp. 248–264). New York: Guilford Press.

Griez, E. & van den Hout, M. A. (1983). Treatment of phobophobia by exposure to CO_2-induced anxiety symptoms. *Journal of Nervous and Mental Diseases, 171*, 506–508.

Halperin, D. M., Weitzman, M. L., & Otto, M. W. (2009). Therapeutic alliance and common factors in treatment. In M. W. Otto & S. G. Hofmann (Eds.), *Avoiding treatment failures in the anxiety disorders* (pp. 51–66). New York: Springer.

Heimberg, R. G. (2001). Current status of psychotherapeutic interventions for social phobia. *Journal of Clinical Psychiatry, 62*(Suppl. 1), 36–42.

Hettema, J. M., Prescott, C. A., & Kendler, K. S. (2001). A population-based twin study of generalized anxiety disorder in men and women. *Journal of Nervous and Mental Disease, 189*, 413–420.

Hofmann, S. G., Barlow, D. H., Papp, L. A., Detweiler, M. F., Ray, S. E., Shear, M. K., Woods, S. W., & Gorman, J. M. (1998). Pretreatment attrition in a comparative treatment outcome study on panic disorder. *American Journal of Psychiatry, 155*, 43–47.

Hofmann, S. G., & Otto, M. W. (2008). *Cognitive behavior therapy for social anxiety disorder: Evidence–based and disorder-specific treatment techniques.* New York: Routledge.

Hollon, S. D. (2001). Behavioral activation treatment for depression: A commentary. *Clinical Psychology: Science and Practice, 8*, 271–274.

Hopko, D. R., Lejuez, C. W., Ruggiero, K. J., & Eifert, G. H. (2003). Contemporary behavioral activation treatments for depression: Procedures, principles, and progress. *Clinical Psychology Review, 23*, 699–717.

Hopko, D. R., Robertson, S. M., & Carvalho, J. P. (2009). Sudden gains in depressed cancer patients treated with behavioral activation therapy. *Behavior Therapy, 40*, 346–356.

Hunot, V., Churchill, R., Teixeira, V., & Silva de Lima, M. (2007). Psychological therapies for generalized anxiety disorder. *Cochrane Database of Systematic Reviews, 1.*

Jacobs, G. D., Pace-Schott, E. F., Stickgold, R., & Otto, M. W. (2004). Cognitive behavior therapy and pharmacotherapy for insomnia: A randomized controlled trial and direct comparison. *Archives of Internal Medicine, 164*, 1888–1896.

Jacobson, N. S., Dobson, K. S., Truax, P. A., Addis, M. E., Koerner, K., Gollan, J. K., et al. (1996). A component analysis of cognitive-behavioral treatment for depression. *Journal of Consulting and Clinical Psychology, 64,* 295–304.

Jacobson, N. S., Martell, C. R., & Dimidjian, S. (2001). Behavioral activation treatment for depression: Returning to contextual roots. *Clinical Psychology: Science and Practice, 8,* 255–270.

Jang, K. L., Stein, M. B., Taylor, S., & Livesley, W. J. (1999). Gender differences in the etiology of anxiety sensitivity: A twin study. *Journal of Gender-Specific Medicine, 2,* 39–44.

Jorm, A. F., Morgan, A. J., & Hetrick, S. E. (2008). Relaxation for depression. *Cochrane Database of Systematic Reviews, 4.*

Kendler, K. S., Neale, M. C., Kessler, R. C., Ronald, C., Heath, A. C., et al. (1993). A longitudinal twin study of personality and major depression in women. *Archives of General Psychiatry, 50,* 853–862.

Kupfer, D. J., & Reynolds, C. F., III (1997). Management of insomnia. *New England Journal of Medicine, 336,* 341–346.

Lejuez, C. W., Hopko, D. R., & Hopko, S. D. (2001). A brief behavioral activation treatment for depression: Treatment manual. *Behavior Modification, 25,* 255–286.

Lejuez, C. W., Zvolensky, M. J., Daughters, S. B., Bornovalova, M. A., Paulson, A., Tull, M. T., et al. (2008). Anxiety sensitivity: A unique predictor of dropout among inner-city heroin and crack/cocaine users in residential substance use treatment. *Behavior Research and Therapy, 46,* 811–818.

Lincoln, T. M., & Rief, W. (2004). How much do sample characteristics affect the effect size? An investigation of studies testing the treatment effects for social phobia. *Journal of Anxiety Disorders, 18,* 515–529.

MacLeod, C. (2004). Information processing approaches to generalized anxiety disorder: Assessing the selective functioning of attention, interpretation, and memory in GAD patients. In R. G. Heimberg, C. L. Turk, & D. S. Mennin (Eds.), *Generalized anxiety disorder: Advances in research and practice* (pp. 77–108). New York: Guilford Press.

MacLeod, C., & Mathews, A. (1991). Biased cognitive operations in anxiety: accessibility of information or assignment of processing priorities? *Behaviour Research and Therapy, 29,* 599–610.

Maier, S. F. & Seligman, M. E. P. (1976). Learned helplessness: Theory and evidence. *Journal of Experimental Psychology: General, 105,* 3–46.

Malcarne, V. L., & Hansdottir, I. (2001). Vulnerability to anxiety disorders in childhood and adolescence. In R. E. Ingram & J. M. Price (Eds.), *Vulnerability to psychopathology: Risk across the lifespan* (pp. 271–303). New York: Guilford Press.

Maltby, N. & Tolin, D. F. (2005). A brief motivational intervention for treatment-refusing OCD patients. *Cognitive and Behaviour Therapy, 34,* 176–184.

Manfro, G. G., Otto, M. W, McArdle, E. T., Worthington, J. J., Rosenbaum, J. F., & Pollack, M. H. (1996). Relationship of antecedent stressful life events to childhood and family history of anxiety and the course of panic disorder. *Journal of Affective Disorders, 41,* 135–139.

Marks, I. M., Swinson, R. P., Basaglu, M., Kuch, K., Nasirvani, H., O'Sullivan, G., Lelliott, P. T., Kirby, M., McNamee, G., Sengun, S., et al (1993). Alprazolam and exposure alone and combined in panic disorder with agoraphobia: A controlled study in London and Toronto. *British Journal of Psychiatry, 162,* 776–787.

Martin, D. J., Garske, J. P., & Davis, M. K. (2000). Relation of the therapeutic alliance with outcome and other variables: A meta-analytic review. *Journal of Consulting and Clinical Psychology, 68*(3), 438–450.

McHugh, R. K., Smits, J. A. J., & Otto, M. W. (2009). Empirically-supported treatments for panic disorder. *Psychiatric Clinics of North America, 32*, 593–610.

McNally, R. J. (2002). Anxiety sensitivity and panic disorder. *Biological Psychiatry, 52*, 938–946.

Mendelson, W. B. (2007). Combining pharmacologic and nonpharmacologic therapies for insomnia. *Journal of Clinical Psychiatry, 68*(Suppl. 5), 19–23.

Morawetz, D. (2003). Insomnia and depression: Which comes first? *Sleep Research Online, 5*, 77–81.

Morgan, K., Dixon, S., Mathers, N., Thompson, J., & Tomeny, M. (2004). Psychological treatment for insomnia in the regulation of long-term hypnotic drug use. *Health Technological Assessment, 8*, 1–68.

Morin, C. M. (2004). Cognitive-behavioral approaches to the treatment of insomnia. *Journal of Clinical Psychiatry, 65*(Suppl. 16), 33–40.

Morin, C. M., Bastien, C., Guay, B., Radouco-Thomas, M., Leblanc, J., & Vallieres, A. (2004). Randomized clinical trial of supervised tapering and cognitive behavior therapy to facilitate benzodiazepine discontinuation in older adults with chronic insomnia. *American Journal of Psychiatry, 161*, 332–342.

Morin, C. M., Bootzin, R. R., Buysse, D. J., Edinger, J. D., Espie, C. A., & Lichstein, K. L. (2006). Psychological and behavioral treatment of insomnia: Update of the recent evidence (1998–2004). *Sleep, 29*, 1398–1414.

Morin, C. M., Colecchi, C., Stone, J., Sood, R., & Brink, D. (1999). Behavioral and pharmacological therapies for late-life insomnia: A randomized controlled trial. *Journal of the American Medical Association, 281*, 991–999.

Morin, C. M., Culbert, J. P., & Schwartz, S. M. (1994). Nonpharmacological interventions for insomnia: a meta-analysis of treatment efficacy. *American Journal of Psychiatry, 151*, 1172–1180.

Morin, C. M., Gaulier, B., Barry, T., & Kowatch, R. A. (1992). Patients' acceptance of psychological and pharmacological therapies for insomnia. *Sleep, 15*, 302–305.

Morin, C. M., Vallieres, A., Guay, B., Ivers, H., Savard, J., Merette, C., et al. (2009). Cognitive behavioral therapy, singly and combined with medication, for persistent insomnia: a randomized controlled trial. *Journal of the American Medical Association, 301*, 2005–2015.

Moscovitch, D. A., Hofmann, S. G., Suvak, M., & In-Albon, T. (2005). Mediation of changes in anxiety and depression during treatment for social phobia. *Journal of Consulting and Clinical Psychology, 73*, 945–952.

Murtagh, D. R., & Greenwood, K. M. (1995). Identifying effective psychological treatments for insomnia: a meta-analysis. *Journal of Consulting and Clinical Psychology, 63*, 79–89.

NHLBI Working Group on Insomnia. (1998). *Insomnia: Assessment and management in primary care.* NIH Publication No. 98–4088.

Ocanez, K. S., McHugh, R. K., & Otto, M. W. (2010). A meta-analytic review of the association between anxiety sensitivity and pain. *Depression and Anxiety, 27*, 760–767.

Otto, M. W. (2000). Stories and metaphors in cognitive-behavior therapy. *Cognitive and Behavioral Practice, 7*, 166–172.

Otto, M. W. (2008) Anxiety sensitivity, emotional intolerance, and expansion of the application of interoceptive exposure: Comment on the special issue. *Journal of Cognitive Psychotherapy, 22*, 379–384.

Otto, M. W., Fava, M., Penava, S. A., Bless, E., Muller, R. T., & Rosenbaum, J. F. (1997). Life event and cognitive predictors of perceived stress before and after treatment for major depression. *Cognitive Therapy and Research, 21,* 409–420.

Otto, M. W., & Hinton, D. E. (2006). Modifying exposure-based CBT for Cambodian refugees with posttraumatic stress disorder. *Cognitive and Behavioral Practice, 13,* 261–270.

Otto, M. W., & Pollack, M. H. (2009). *Stopping anxiety medication* (Therapist guide, 2nd ed.). New York: Oxford University Press.

Otto, M. W., Reilly-Harrington, N. A., Kogan, J. N., Henin, A., Knauz, R. O., & Sachs, G. S. (2009). *Managing bipolar disorder: A cognitive-behavioral approach* (Therapist guide). New York: Oxford University Press.

Otto, M. W., & Smits, J. A. J. (2009). *Exercise for mood and anxiety disorders (Workbook).* New York: Oxford University Press.

Otto, M. W., Smits, J. A. J., & Reese, H. E. (2005). Combined psychotherapy and pharmacotherapy for mood and anxiety disorders in adults: Review and analysis. *Clinical Psychology: Science and Practice, 12,* 72–86.

Perlis, M. L., Jungquist, C., Smith, M. T., & Posner, D. (2005). *Cognitive behavioral treatment of insomnia: A session-by-session guide.* New York: Springer.

Peterson, C., & Seligman, M. E. P. (1984). Causal explanations as a risk factor for depression: Theory and evidence. *Psychological Review, 91,* 347–374.

Pollack, M., Kinrys, G., Krystal, A., McCall, W. V., Roth, T., Schaefer, K., et al. (2008). Eszopiclone coadministered with escitalopram in patients with insomnia and comorbid generalized anxiety disorder. *Archives of General Psychiatry, 65,* 551–562.

Powers, M. B., Smits, J. A., & Telch, M. J. (2004). Disentangling the effects of safety-behavior utilization and safety-behavior availability during exposure-based treatment: a placebo-controlled trial. *Journal of Consulting and Clinical Psychology, 72*(3), 448–454.

Powers, M. B., Smits, J. A. J., Whitley, D., Bystritsky, A., & Telch, M. J. (2008). The effect of attributional processes concerning medication taking on return of fear. *Journal of Consulting and Clinical Psychology, 76,* 478–490.

Powers, M. B., Vervliet, B., Smits, J. A. J., & Otto, M. W. (2010). Helping exposure succeed: Learning theory perspectives on treatment resistance and relapse. In M. W. Otto & S. G. Hofmann (Eds.), *Avoiding treatment failures in the anxiety disorders* (pp. 31–49). New York: Springer.

Reynolds, C. F., III, Frank, E., Houck, P. R., Mazumdar, S., Dew, M. A., Cornes, C., et al. (1997). Which elderly patients with remitted depression remain well with continued interpersonal psychotherapy after discontinuation of antidepressant medication? *American Journal of Psychiatry, 154,* 958–962.

Ritterband, L. M., Thorndike, F. P., Gonder-Frederick, L. A., Magee, J. C., Bailey, E. T., Saylor, D. K., et al. (2009). Efficacy of an Internet-based behavioral intervention for adults with insomnia. *Archives of General Psychiatry, 66,* 692–698.

Roemer, L., Molina, S., & Borkovec, T. D. (1997). An investigation of worry content among generally anxious individuals. *Journal of Nervous and Mental Disease, 185,* 314–319.

Rottenberg, J., Gross, J. J., & Gotlieb, I. H. (2005). Emotional context insensitivity in major depressive disorder. *Journal of Abnormal Psychology, 114,* 627–639.

Ruini, C. & Fava, G. A. (2009). Well-being therapy for generalized anxiety disorder. *Journal of Clinical Psychology, 65,* 510–519.

Salkovskis, P. M., Clark, D. M., & Gelder, M. G. (1996). Cognitive-behavior links in the persistence of panic. *Behaviour Research and Therapy, 34*, 453–458.

Schmidt, N. B., Woolaway-Bickel, K., Trakowski, J., Santiago, H., Storey, J., Koselka, M., et al. (2000). Dismantling cognitive-behavioral treatment for panic disorder: Questioning the utility of breathing retraining. *Journal of Consulting and Clinical Psychology, 68(3)*, 417–424.

Seligman, M. E. P. (1975). *Helplessness: On depression, development, and death.* San Francisco: W. H. Freeman.

Semler, C. N., & Harvey, A. G. (2005). Misperception of sleep can adversely affect daytime functioning in insomnia. *Behaviour Research and Therapy, 43*, 843–856.

Shuman AL, Shapiro JP. (2002). The effects of preparing parents for child psychotherapy on accuracy of expectations and treatment attendance. *Community Mental Health Journal, 38*, 3–16.

Siev, J., & Chambless, D. L. (2007). Specificity of treatment effects: Cognitive therapy and relaxation for generalized anxiety and panic disorders. *Journal of Consulting and Clinical Psychology, 75*, 513–522.

Simon N. M., Weiss, A. M., Kradin, R., Evans, K. C., Reese, H. E., et al. (2006). The relationship of anxiety disorders, anxiety sensitivity and pulmonary dysfunction with dyspnea related distress and avoidance. *Journal of Nervous and Mental Disease, 194*, 951–957.

Sloan, D. M., Bradley, M. M., Dimoulas, E., & Lang, P. J. (2002). Looking at facial expressions: Dysphoria and facial EMG. *Biological Psychology, 60*, 79–90.

Smith, M. T., Huang, M. I., & Manber, R. (2005). Cognitive behavior therapy for chronic insomnia occurring within the context of medical and psychiatric disorders. *Clinical Psychology Review, 25*, 559–592.

Smith, M. T., Perlis, M. L., Park, A., Smith, M. S., Pennington, J., Giles, D. E., et al. (2002). Comparative meta-analysis of pharmacotherapy and behavior therapy for persistent insomnia. *American Journal of Psychiatry, 159*, 5–11.

Stathopoulou, G., Powers, M. B., Berry, A. C., Smits, J. A. J., & Otto, M. W. (2006). Exercise interventions for mental health: A quantitative and qualitative review. *Clinical Psychology: Science and Practice, 13*, 179–193.

Tang, T. Z., & DeRubeis, R. J. (1999). Sudden gains and critical sessions in cognitive-behavioral therapy for depression. *Journal of Consulting and Clinical Psychology, 67*, 894–904.

Tang, T. Z., Derubeis, R. J., Hollon, S. D., Amsterdam, J., & Shelton, R. (2007). Sudden gains in cognitive therapy of depression and depression relapse/recurrence. *Journal of Consulting and Clinical Psychology, 75*, 404–408.

Taylor, D. J., Lichstein, K. L., Weinstock, J., Sanford, S., & Temple, J. R. (2007). A pilot study of cognitive-behavioral therapy of insomnia in people with mild depression. *Behavior Therapy, 38*, 49–57.

Teasdale, J. D., Moore, R. G., Hayhurst, H., Pope, M., Williams, S., Segal, Z. V. (2002). Metacognitive awareness and prevention of relapse in depression: empirical evidence. *Journal of Consulting and Clinical Psychology, 70*, 275–287.

Telch, M. J. (1988). Combined pharmacological and psychological treatments for panic sufferers. In S. Rachman & J. D. Maser (Eds.), *Panic: Psychological perspectives* (pp. 167–187). Hillsdale, NJ: Erlbaum.

Thase, M. E. (1999). Antidepressant treatment of the depressed patient with insomnia. *Journal of Clinical Psychiatry, 60*(Suppl. 17), 28–31.

Thorp, S. R., Ayers, C. R., Nuevo, R., Stoddard, J. A., Sorrell, J. T., & Wetherell, J. L. (2009). Meta-analysis comparing different behavioral treatments for late-life anxiety. *American Journal of Geriatric Psychiatry, 17,* 105–115.

Trivedi, M. H., Greer, T. L., Grannemann, B. D., Chambliss, H. O., & Jordan, A. N. (2006). Exercise as an augmentation strategy for treatment of major depression. *Journal of Psychiatric Practice, 12,* 205–213.

Vallieres, A., Morin, C. M., & Guay, B. (2005). Sequential combinations of drug and cognitive behavioral therapy for chronic insomnia: An exploratory study. *Behaviour Research and Therapy, 43,* 1611–1630.

Van der Heiden, C., & ten Broeke, E. (2009). The when, why, and how of worry exposure. *Cognitive and Behavioral Practice, 16,* 386–393.

Vincent, N., & Lewycky, S. (2009). Logging on for better sleep: RCT of the effectiveness of online treatment for insomnia. *Sleep, 32,* 807–815.

Vincent, N., & Lionberg, C. (2001). Treatment preference and patient satisfaction in chronic insomnia. *Sleep, 24,* 411–417.

Wells, A., Clark, D. M., Salkovskis, P., Ludgate, J., Hackmann, A., & Gelder, M. (1995). Social phobia: The role of in-situation safety behaviors in maintaining anxiety and negative beliefs. *Behavior Therapy, 26,* 153–161.

Wells, A., & Papageorgiou, C. (1998). Social phobia: Effects of external attention on anxiety, negative beliefs, and perspective taking. *Behavior Therapy, 29,* 357–370.

Westra, H. A., Dozois, D. J., & Marcus, M. (2007). Expectancy, homework compliance, and initial change in cognitive-behavioral therapy for anxiety. *Journal of Consulting and Clinical Psychology, 75,* 363–373.

Williams, J. M. G., Barnhofer, T., Crane, C., & Beck, A. T. (2005). Problem solving deteriorates following mood challenge in formerly depressed patients with a history of suicidal ideation. *Journal of Abnormal Psychology, 114,* 421–431.

Winokur, A., & Reynolds, C. F., III. (1994). The effects of antidepressants on sleep physiology. *Primary Psychiatry, 1,* 22–27.

Woods, C. M., Chambless, D. L., & Steketee, G. (2002). Homework compliance and behavior therapy outcome for panic with agoraphobia and obsessive compulsive disorder. *Cognitive Behaviour Therapy, 31,* 88–95.

Woody, S., McLean, P. D., Taylor, S., & Koch, W. (1999). Treatment of major depression in the context of panic disorder. *Journal of Affective Disorders, 53,* 163–174.

Zavesicka, L., Brunovsky, M., Matousek, M., & Sos, P. (2008). Discontinuation of hypnotics during cognitive behavioural therapy for insomnia. *BMC Psychiatry, 8,* 80.

Zimbarg, R. E., Craske, M. G., & Barlow, D. H. (2006). *Mastery of your anxiety and worry* (Therapist Guide, 2nd ed.). New York: Oxford University Press.

Zou, J. B., Hudson, J. L., & Rapee, R. M. (2007). The effect of attentional focus on social anxiety. *Behaviour Research and Therapy, 45,* 2326–2333.

INDEX

accurate thoughts, 23
achievement activities, 40
activity
  current, monitored, 93–94
  goal-directed, 75
  hierarchy, 96–97, 96t
  patterns of, 40
  Planned Activity List and, 95, 95t, 157t
  valued, increasing, 78
activity assignments
  achievement activities in, 40
  for anxiety disorders, 28–31
  for depression, 40
  emotional tolerance and, 29–33
  exercise, 41–43
  for mood disorders, 28
  planning checklist for, 39f, 69, 75, 157f
  pleasant events, 40–41
  self-monitoring form for, 40
  Steps to Goal Attainment form
    and, 40, 97, 158f
  Weekly Activity Schedule
    and, 40–41, 153t
additive model of phobic concern, 33–34
aerobic exercise, recommendations
  for, 42
affective disorders, insomnia and, 137
alcohol abuse, 147
alliance, therapeutic, 7
all-or-nothing thinking, 17, 17t, 152
amplifying cognitions, 17
anxiety disorders. *See also* generalized anxiety
  disorder; panic disorder; social anxiety
  disorder
  activity assignments for, 28–31
  cognitive interventions for, 19–23, 44,
    57–63, 103–06, 119–22, 120t

exercise for, 41
exposure assignments for, 28–31
relaxation and, 49113
thought monitoring for, 19–23, 24f
Anxiety Sensitivity Index, 56
anxiogenic thoughts, common, 55, 55t, 162
assignments. *See* activity assignments
attributional style, learned
  helplessness and, 89
avoidance
  acceptance and, 29
  active, 119
  passive, 119
  patterns of, 40
  worry and, 102, 111

BA. *See* behavioral activation
Beck, A. T., 24
Beckian cognitive therapy, 16
behavioral activation (BA)
  activity hierarchy and, 96–97, 96t
  clinician/patient dialogues and, 92–97
  current activities monitored in, 93–94
  depression and, 91–98, 95t–96t
  potential activities identified
    in, 94–95, 95t
  progress monitoring and, 97
  rationale provided in, 92–93
  steps, 91
  theoretical foundation, 91–92
  treatments, 40, 41
behavioral experiments, 15
benzodiazepines, 72, 141–42, 145–46, 149
bipolar disorder, 17–18
black-and-white thinking. *See* all-or-nothing
  thinking
borderline personality disorder, 31

ABOUT THE AUTHORS

Michael W. Otto, Ph.D., is Professor of Psychology and Director of the Translational Research Program at the Center for Anxiety and Related Disorders at Boston University.

Naomi M. Simon, M.D., is Associate Director of the Center for Anxiety and Traumatic Stress Disorders at Massachusetts General Hospital, and Associate Professor of Psychiatry at Harvard Medical School.

Bunmi O. Olatunji, Ph.D., is Associate Professor of Psychology at Vanderbilt University.

Sharon C. Sung, Ph.D., is Assistant Professor at the Duke-NUS Graduate Medical School in Singapore.

Mark H. Pollack, M.D., is Professor of Psychiatry and Director of the Center for Anxiety and Traumatic Stress Disorders at Massachusetts General Hospital and Harvard Medical School.